KITCHIN'S MAP OF SHETLAND, 1751.

En hanseatisk Bergensfarer fra ca. 1650.

Tyskebryggen i Bergen.

SCOTS-SCANDINAVIAN LINKS IN EUROPE AND AMERICA, 1550–1850

By
David Dobson

CLEARFIELD

Printed for
Clearfield Company, Inc. by
Genealogical Publishing Co., Inc.
Baltimore, Maryland
2005

International Standard Book Number: 0-8063-5269-8

Made in the United States of America

Scots-Scandinavian Links, 1550-1850

Introduction

During the sixteenth and seventeenth centuries there was significant emigration, both permanent and temporary, from Scotland to the Scandinavian lands of Norway, Sweden and Denmark. Some of this was by economic migrants, especially merchants and craftsmen, in search of career opportunities, but the majority of Scots went as soldiers of fortune seeking employment in the armies of Sweden and Norway-Denmark under leaders such as Gustavus Adolphus. Many of those who arrived as soldiers and survived campaigns such as the Thirty Years War were granted land and encouraged to settle. The merchants and craftsmen who emigrated to Scandinavia generally originated from burghs along the east coast of Scotland and from as far north as the Orkney and Shetland Islands. In Stockholm there were many Scottish goldsmiths and silversmiths; one Blasius Dundee acted as banker to the Swedish king in the late sixteenth century. Soldiers were recruited from all parts of Scotland, though some regiments such as Colonel Robert Munro's or Lord Reay's were mainly recruited for in the northern Highlands. On the outbreak of the Bishop's War in 1638, the start of the Wars of the Three Kingdoms, many of the Scottish soldiers returned home from Scandinavia to provide the backbone of the Covenanter Army that successfully opposed the forces of King Charles I. The Swedish and Danish kings not only recruited soldiers from Scotland but also seafarers. Experienced Scots seafarers were employed in various capacities; for example, John Cunningham led a naval expedition to Greenland and Labrador in 1605. Later he became governor of Vardohus and Finmark in northern Norway. Several of the Admirals of the Swedish Navy belonged to the Scottish Clerck family. Sanders Clerck took part in the Swedish expedition to the Delaware in 1638, while Richard Clerck acted as commissary of the Swedish West India Company around 1646.

The failure of the Jacobites in 1715 and in 1746 caused a number of them seek refuge in Sweden; some—such as the

Carnegies—became burghers of Gothenburg. This city had attracted Scots immigrants since it was developed in the seventeenth century. The city was home to the Swedish East Indian Company, which was created around 1730 to rival the English and the Dutch East India Companies. One of its more prominent employees was Colin Campbell, who was sent to China in 1731 to establish trading links. The industrialization of Gothenburg in the nineteenth century was facilitated by Scottish entrepreneurs such as James Dickson, William Gibson and Alexander Keillor.

In the early modern period, tens of thousands of Scots settled in Scandinavia, some permanently and others temporarily. Some of them, or their descendants, were involved in trade and settlement in the Americas. A handful of Scots were engaged in the Swedish Settlements on the Delaware as colonists, seafarers, or merchants based in Sweden and trading in colonial produce. Far more Scots were noted as planters and merchants in the Danish West Indian colony of the Virgin Islands—St. Jan, St. Thomas and St. Croix—during the eighteenth and nineteenth centuries. How the Scots got to the Virgin Islands is not clear. There is no evidence of any direct shipping links between Scotland until the latter eighteenth century when ships bringing cargoes of cotton and other colonial produce appear in the records of some west of Scotland ports. Some Scots may have emigrated via Copenhagen, while others may have settled there after the American Revolution. The story of the Scots in the Virgin Islands has yet to be researched. For those interested in the Scots in Scandinavia, the most recent books are Steve Murdoch's *Britain, Denmark-Norway and the House of Stuart, 1603–1660* (Tuckwell Press, 2000); Thomas Riis's *Should Auld Acquaintance Be Forgot...Scottish-Danish Relations 1450–1707* (Odense University Press, 1988); and Jonas Berg and Bo Lagercrantz's *Scots in Sweden* (The Swedish Institute, 1962).

David Dobson
St Andrews, Scotland, 2005

Johannes Magnus's Kart over Norden. Fra Beg. af 16de Aarhundrede.

Highland Troops in Swedish service in 1631.

Stockholms slott vid slutet af 1600-talet.

REFERENCES

ARCHIVES

AA	=	Angus Archives, Montrose
NAS	=	National Archives of Scotland, Edinburgh
PRO	=	Public Record Office, London
RAK	=	Rigs Arkivet, Kobenhavn, Denmark
SAB	=	Stadsarkivet, Bergen, Norway
SAM	=	Stadsarkivet, Malmo, Sweden.

PUBLICATIONS

ABR	=	Ayr Burgess Roll
AJ	=	Aberdeen Journal, series
BM	=	Blackwood's Edinburgh Magazine, series
CFR	=	Cockburn Family Records, R. Cockburn, [Edinburgh, 1913]
DFI	=	The Danish Force in Ireland, 1690-1691, [Dublin, 1962]
DPCA		Dundee, Perth & Cupar Advertiser, series
EA	=	Edinburgh Advertiser, series
EBR	=	Edinburgh Burgh Records
EEC	=	Edinburgh Evening Courant, series
FH	=	Fife Herald, series
GC	=	Glasgow Courier, series
GM	=	Gentleman's Magazine, series
JSL	=	John Stewart's Letterbook, 1715-1752, [Edinburgh, 1915]
MD	=	Mudies of Dundee ..., J. H. Mudie, [Florida, 2000]
NS	=	Northern Scotland, series
SAS	=	Scotland and Scandinavia, 800-1800, [Edinburgh, 1990]
SBL	=	Svenskt Biografiskt Lexicon, [Stockholm, 1927]
SE	=	Scotland and Europe, 1200-1850, [Edinburgh1986]
SHR	=	Scottish Historical Review, series
SIS	=	Scots in Sweden, Stockholm, 1962
SM	=	Scots Magazine, series
SP	=	Scots Peerage, [Edinburgh, 1908]
SS	=	Surnames of Scotland, [New York, 1946]

ST = Scots Times, series
W = Witness, series

Example of a Birth Brief

*"The said day [16 October 1628] In Presens of the Shref deput
forsaid Comperit Johne Watson in Crabstoun James Thome
thair Walter Sklett in Sklettie & Richart Watsone burgess of
Abd and being sworne deponit that they knew umqll Johne
Gordoun merchand & traveller within the dominion and
kingdome of Swain within the Toun of Copperberrie To
haive bein sone natural repute & haldin & procreat betuixt
Johne Gordoun sumtyme of Lastis now of Craibstoun and
Elspet Keyth his mother and brother on the father syd
procreat as said is to James Gordoun fiar of Craibstoun
eldest lawfull sone to the said Johne Gordoun of Craibstoun
Quairunto the Shref deput of Abd Interponit his authoritie
And thairupon Thomas Merser notar publict in Auld Abd in
name of the said James Gordoun tuik Act & Instrument.*

Mr Andersone   Mr Alexr. Paip
Shreffe Clark of Abd   Shreff deput

Source: Aberdeen Sheriff Court, Judicial Enactments, Vol.IV

SCOTS-SCANDINAVIAN LINKS IN EUROPE AND AMERICA, 1550-1850

ADAM, Reverend Dr ROBERT, in St Croix, Danish West Indies, 1821. [NAS.RD5.204.550]

ADAMSON, JOHN, a cooper from Orkney, admitted as a burgess of Bergen, Norway, in 1642. [SAB]

AITKEN, CHARLES, 'born in North Britain', a merchant in St Croix, married Cornelia Beekman in New York on 22 August 1771, died in St Croix, Danish West Indies, in May 1784, a planter in St Croix, probate 1815 PCC, brother of Reverend John Aitken in St Vigeans, Angus. [NAS.RD5.92.723][ANY.I.128][PRO.PCC.prob.37/297]

AITKEN, GEORGE, in St Croix, Danish West Indies, 1795, brother of Reverend John Aitken in St Vigeans, Angus. [NAS.RD5.92.723]; a planter in St Croix, 1815. [PRO.Probate 37/297]

AITKEN, JANE, daughter of the late Charles Aitken in St Croix, married James Mudie, London, in North Tarry, Angus, on 11 December 1798. [AJ#2660]

AITKEN, ROBERT, probate December 1767 Christiansted, Danish West Indies. [RAK]

AITKEN, WILLIAM, in Bergen, Norway, son of David Aitken a merchant in Kirkwall, Orkney in 1630. [NAS.RS43.4.121]

ALBERTSON, ALBERT, from Orkney, admitted as a burgess of Bergen, Norway, in 1614. [SAB]

ALBERTSON, GILBERT, from Orkney, a burgess of Bergen, Norway, in 1617. [POAS.XII.39][SAB]

ALBERTSON, PETER, (Peder Albritsen), from Orkney, admitted
as a burgess of Bergen, Norway, in 1621.
[SAB][POAS.XII.39]

ALBERTSON, PETER, a weaver from Orkney, admitted as a
burgess of Bergen, Norway, in 1644. [SAB]

ALBERTSON, THOMAS, from Leith, a burgess of Bergen,
Norway, in 1641. [SAB]

ALEXANDER, JOHN, son of James Alexander and his wife
Marjory Douglas in Mounie, Daviot, admitted as a burgess of
Malmo, Denmark, in 1593. [MSC.II.22]

ALGERON, GUSTAVE, Baron de Stjerneld, born 1791 in
Stockholm, Sweden, arrived via Stockton, residing in
Edinburgh by 1807. [ECA.SL115.2.2/57]

ALLAN, ALEXANDER, from Orkney, admitted as a burgess of
Bergen, Norway, in 1625. [SAB]

ALLAN, GAVIN, an officer of Mackay's Regiment, in Danish
service 1626, then in Swedish service 1629. [TGSI.VIII.188]

ALLAN, GEORGE, in St Croix, possibly from Edinburgh, a partner
in the firm of Allan, Walker and Company, died on 18 June
1820, nephew of Reverend Alexander, an Episcopalian
minister in Edinburgh. [NAS.RD5.168.283; 301.447]
[NAS.SH.1820][BM#7/594][EEC#16615][EA#5904]
[NAS.B22.4.21/22]

ALLAN, ROBERT, probate 14 June 1775 Christiansted, Danish
West Indies. [RAK:CCLVII/271]

ALLEN, JAMES, from Scotland, a burgess of Bergen, Norway, in
1650. [SAB]

ALLEN, JOHN, from Queensferry, West Lothian, a burgess of
Bergen, Norway, in 1692. [SAB]

ANDERSON, ADAM, from Orkney, a burgess of Bergen, Norway,
in 1614.   [POAS.XII.39]

ANDERSON, ADAM, from Orkney, admitted as a burgess of Bergen, Norway, in 1623. [SAB]

ANDERSON, ALBERT, from Orkney, a burgess of Bergen, Norway, in 1614. [POAS.XII.39]

ANDERSON, ANDREAS, master of the <u>Christian and Karen of Trontheim</u>, from Greenock to St Thomas, Danish West Indies, in September 1782. [NAS.E504.15.36]

ANDERSON, ANDREW, a cooper from Lybster (?), (Lester), a burgess of Bergen, Norway, in 1636. [SAB]

ANDERSON, ANDREW, from Orkney, admitted as a burgess of Bergen, Norway, in 1643. [SAB]

ANDERSON, JAMES, from Fraserburgh, Aberdeenshire, was admitted as a burgess of Bergen, Norway, in 1618. [SAB]

ANDERSON, JAMES, from Scotland, admitted as a burgess of Bergen, Norway, in 1623. [SAB]

ANDERSON, JAMES, from Scotland, a burgess of Bergen, Norway, in 1634. [SAB]

ANDERSON, JAMES, in St Croix, Danish West Indies, 1790. [Caribbeana#5/265]

ANDERSON, JANE, only daughter of John Anderson in St Croix, married George Anderson a surgeon in Stirling, there on 8 December 1817. [BM.II.473]

ANDERSON, JOHN, from Scotland, admitted as a burgess of Bergen, Norway, in 1615. [SAB]

ANDERSON, JOHN, in St Croix, Danish West Indies, 1790. [Caribbeana#5/265]

ANDERSON, JOSEPH, probate 22 June 1767 Christiansted, Danish West Indies. [RAK]

ANDERSON, LAURENCE, born in 1845, youngest son of William Anderson a wood merchant in Kincardine on Forth, died in Sundvall, Sweden, on 3 October 1884. [S#12870]

ANDERSON, LAURTS, a merchant in Christianna, Norway, in 1684. [NAS.RD2.63.5]

ANDERSON, OLIVER, from Orkney, admitted as a burgess of Bergen, Norway, in 1636. [SAB]

ANDERSON, PETER, from St Andrews, Fife, admitted as a burgess of Bergen, Norway, in 1618. [SAB]

ANDERSON, ROBERT, a leather worker from Orkney, admitted as a burgess of Bergen, Norway, in 1659. [SAB]

ANDERSON, ROBERT, died on 9 March 1824, probate St Jan, Danish West Indies. [RAK: {1807-1826}, fo.131]

ANDERSON, THOMAS, a merchant in Stockholm, Sweden, died in 1672. [SHR.XXV.292]

ANDERSON, WILLIAM, son of Alexander Anderson and his wife Catherine Goudis in Petindrum, settled in Norway by March 1626. Aberdeen birthbrief. [ABL.I.244]

ANDERSON, WILLIAM, from Orkney, admitted as a burgess of Bergen, Norway, in 1647. [SAB]

ANDERSON, WILLIAM, late in St Croix, died in Lenzie, Dunbartonshire, on 11 October 1878. [EC#29343]

ANDREW, RICHARD, probate 13 October 1779 Christiansted, Danish West Indies. [RAK: CCC.XXV.364]

ANDREW, ROBERT, a weaver in Copenhagen, Denmark, son of Robert Andrew and his wife Euphame Mackie in Myreton of Brychty, Angus,1608. [Dundee Archives, CBIII/73]

ARBUCKLE, R. JAMES, probate 26 November 1777, Christianstad, Danish West Indies. [RAK:CCCXXXIV.188]

ARBUTHNOTT, ARTHUR, a Lieutenant of Mackay's Regiment, in Danish service 1626, in Swedish service 1629, wounded at Stralsund. [TGSI.VIII.187]

ARBUTHNOTT, JAMES CARNEGY, born 1740, a merchant in Gothenburg, Sweden, during 1760s, later an innkeeper, died 1810. [SE#117][SIS#63]

ARMISS, ..., a Captain of Mackay's Regiment, in Danish service 1626, in Swedish service 1629, wounded at Stralsund. [TGSI.VIII.187]

ARMSTRONG, EDWARD, in St Croix, Danish West Indies, 1790. Caribbeana#5/265]

ARMSTRONG, MARTHA, died 11 November 1844, probate St Jan, Danish West Indies. [RAK: 1835-1842, fo.42]

ARMSTRONG, THOMAS, in St Croix, Danish West Indies, 1790. [Caribbeana#5/265]

ARMSTRONG, THOMAS T., in St Croix, Danish West Indies, 1790. [Caribbeana#5/265]

ARMSTRONG, WILLIAM, in St Croix, Danish West Indies, 1801. [NLS.MS5602/3]

AYRES, ROBERT, in St Thomas, Danish West Indies, probate 1780 PCC [PRO.458/Collins]

BAILLIE, DAVID, in St Croix, Danish West Indies, probate 1797 PCC. [PRO.631, Exeter]

BAIRD, ROBERT, probate 20 July 1774 Christiansted, Danish West Indies, [RAK: XIX.302]

BALFOUR, M. Y., Lieutenant of the 96th Regiment, died in St Croix during 1808. [EA#4698]

BALLANTYNE, Dr GEORGE, died in Gothenburg, Sweden, during February 1770. [SM.xxxii.397]

BANNERMAN, ALEXANDER, of Elsick, son of Sir Alexander Bannerman and his wife Isabella Macdonald, Jacobite Colonel in 1746, escaped to Norway in November 1746, settled in Gothenburg, Sweden. [SHR.lxx.63]

BARBOUR, ..., a Lieutenant of Mackay's Regiment, in Danish service 1626, in Swedish service 1629, killed at Brandenburg. [TGSI.VIII.187]

BARCLAY, ANDREW, born in Scotland during 1791, a Presbyterian, settled as a planter on Grange Estate, St Croix, Danish West Indies, by 1841. [1841 Census]

BARCLAY, GEORGE, from Aberdeen, a burgess of Bergen, Norway, in 1643. [SAB]

BARCLAY, JACOBINA CAMPBELL, youngest daughter of James Barclay in Port Glasgow, married Reverend Henry Scott, in Gothenburg, Sweden, on 28 April 1846. [EEC#21344]

BARCLAY, MARY CAMPBELL, eldest daughter of James Barclay in Port Glasgow, married Peter Hammarberg, in Gothenburg, Sweden, on 28 April 1846. [EEC#21344]

BARCLAY, ROBERT, a member of Prince Charles Edward Stuart's Guard, a Jacobite in 1746, settled in Gothenburg, Sweden, by 1747. [SHR.lxx.63]

BARCLAY, SUSANNE, probate 31 August 1774, Christiansted, Danish West Indies. [RAK:CC.XXXII.225]

BARCLAY, THOMAS THOMSON, a shipmaster from Montrose, Angus, applied to become a burgess of Bergen, Norway, in 1708. [SAB]

BARRY, DANIEL, probate 28 July 1777, Christiansted, Danish West Indies. [RAK: CCL.II.24]

BARRY, JOHN, probate 31 March 1779, Christiansted, Danish West Indies. [RAK: CCC.XXII.142]

BARRY, JOHN JAMES, probate 11 December 1759, Christiansted, Danish West Indies. [RAK]

BEATON, JOHN, ('Jan Bieton'), on St Thomas? Danish West Indies, during 1690s. [RAK]

BEATOUN, ..., a Captain of Mackay's Regiment, in Danish service 1626, in Swedish service 1629, wounded at Stralsund. [TGSI.VIII.187]

BEGG, THOMAS, a merchant in Bergen, Norway, son of Magnus Begg and his wife Margaret Mowat in Gossigar, South Ronaldsay, Orkney, 1625. [NAS.RS43.3.140; E108.13]

BELFRAGE, JOHN, born 1614 in Kirkcaldy, Fife, emigrated to Sweden in 1624, later a merchant and burgomaster of Venersborg, enobled in 1666. [SHR.XXV.291]

BELL, PETER, from Bo'ness, West Lothian, a burgess of Bergen, Norway, in 1675. [SAB]

BELL, THOMAS, a printseller in Malmo, was buried in St Peter's, Malmo, Sweden, on 30 September 1617. [SAM]

BELL, THOMAS, probate 1767 Christiansted, Danish West Indies. [RAK.II.2]

BELLENDEN, GEORGE, born in Aberdeen 1718, a medical student, then surgeon of the Swedish East India Company in 1740s, later a merchant in Gothenburg, Sweden, and by 1752 a burgess there, married Sarah Chambers during 1747, died in Gothenburg on 5 February 1770. [SE#117] [AUR#42.40][NS#7.1.145][Goteborgs Landsarkivet, 1755]

BENNET, JOHN, probate 3 April 1762 Christiansted, Danish West Indies. [RAK]

BEVERIDGE, WILLIAM, born 1842, son of Alexander Beveridge and his wife Isabella Pringle, died on St Thomas, Danish West Indies, on 24 August 1865. [Dunnikier, Fife, g/s]

BIRNY, ALEXANDER, son of Alexander Birny a burgess of Aberdeen and his wife Catherine Bishop, settled in Denmark by 1595. [MSC.II.32]

BIRSAY, JAMES, a burgess of Bergen, Norway, son of William Birsay an udaller in Greeny, Orkney, 1625. [NAS.RS43.III.3]

BLACK, GILBERT, sawmiller on Sauda Fjord, Norway, around 1615. [SAS#104]

BLACKADDER, ADAM, born in Troqueer during 16..., son of Reverend John Blackadder (died 1686) and his wife Janet Haining, a merchant in Sweden. [F.2.302]

BLACKWELL, Dr ALEXANDER, born 1700, a physician and animal breeder in Aberdeen, settled in Sweden in 1742 as physician to Frederick I, executed in Stockholm in 1747. [SIS#61][SM.XI.206][SAS#119]

BLAIN, JAMES, in St Thomas, Danish West Indies, 1817. [NAS.SH.1817]

BLAIR, ALEXANDER, a writer in Edinburgh, a Jacobite in 1745, escaped on the .... of North Ferry of Dundee, Captain James Wemyss, from Lunan Bay, Montrose, to Norway, landed in Bergen on 13 May 1746. [CM#3997]

BLAIR, DAVID, born 1793, son of John Blair a calenderer in Glasgow, died in St Croix, Danish West Indies, on 3 February 1816. [Ramshorn g/s, Glasgow]

BLAIR, JOHN, ('Jan Blaer'), on St Thomas, Danish West Indies, 1690s.

BLAIR, THOMAS, a merchant from Dundee, a Jacobite Colonel of the Atholl Regiment in 1745, escaped on the .... of North Ferry of Dundee, Captain James Wemyss, from Lunan Bay, Montrose, to Norway, landed in Bergen on 13 May 1746, settled in Gothenburg, Sweden, by 1747. [SHR.lxx.63][CM#3997]

BODELSON, GEORGE, from Shetland, a burgess of Bergen, Norway, in 1621. [POAS.XIII.39]

BORTHWICK, ELEAZER, in Gothenburg, Sweden, 1637.
[NAS.GD406.1.368/9278]

BOURKE, WILLIAM, born in St Croix, Danish West Indies, a
medical student in Edinburgh 1791-. [ECA.Aliens Register]

BOYD, DAVID, surgeon in the service of the Danish East India
Company, testament confirmed on 10 September 1802 with
the Commissariat of Edinburgh. [NAS]

BOYD, GEORGE, a clerk in St Croix, Danish West Indies, 1784.
[NAS.RD3.244.530]

BOYLE, JAMES LAWRENCE, son of John Boyle in St Croix,
Danish West Indies, 1777. [NAS.SH.1777]; a merchant in St
Croix, 1779, [NAS.CS16.1.175]; 1800, [NAS.CS17.1.19,
350]

BOYLE, JAMES LAWRENCE, son of John Boyle, a merchant in
St Croix, Danish West Indies, 1779, [NAS.CS16.1.175],
1800, [NAS.CS17.1.19/350]

BOYLE, Dr JOHN, probate 6 November 1763 Christiansted,
Danish West Indies. [RAK]

BOYLE, THOMAS, probate 28 November 1781 Christiansted,
Danish West Indies. [RAK.CCCL.XX.147]

BRADNER, ALEXANDER, probate 17 November 1781
Christiansted, Danish West Indies. [RAK C.XII.339]

BREBNER, ALEXANDER, son of John Brebner and his wife May
Davidson in Peterhead, Aberdeenshire, a merchant in St
Croix, Danish West Indies, died there before 1775.
[APB#4/65]

BROWN, ADAM, probate 5 February 1762 Christiansted, Danish
West Indies. [RAK]

BROWN, JAMES, probate 13 June 1766 Christiansted, Danish
West Indies. [RAK]

BROWN, JAMES, a merchant in St Croix, Danish West Indies, married Miss Krause, daughter of Colonel Krause in Danish Service, in St Croix on 23 May 1820. [BM#7/583][S#4/184]; a merchant in Christiansted, Danish West Indies, 1821. [NAS.RD5.204.550]

BROWN, JEAN, daughter of John Brown and his wife Jean Westland in Midmar, Aberdeenshire, emigrated to Philadelphia in 1743, moved to Barbados and later St Croix, wife of Daniel Aspinall, died in St Croix, Danish West Indies, during 1758. [Aberdeen Propinquity Book, #3/202]

BROWN, JOHN, probate 22 May 1767 Christiansted, Danish West Indies. [RAK]

BROWN, Dr PATRICK, probate 1 February 1767 Christiansted, Danish West Indies. [RAK XXX.VII]

BRUCE, THOMAS, a farmer at Topnes, Nedstrand, near Stavanger, Norway, around 1616. [SAS#104]

BRUMFIELD, ..., a Lieutenant of Mackay's Regiment, in Danish service 1626, in Swedish service 1629, promoted in Ruthven's Regiment. [TGSI.VIII.187]

BRUUN, JENS, born 1777 in Dram, Norway, a merchant, arrived in Gravesend on 23 September 1803, residing at Turf's Coffee House, Edinburgh, by 22 November 1803. [ECA.SL115.2.2/23]

BUCHANAN, JAMES, late of St Thomas, Danish West Indies, a burgess of Montrose, Angus, in 1783. [Montrose Burgess Roll]

BUCHANAN, J. S., in St Croix, Danish West Indies, 1790. [Caribbena#5/265]

BUIST, ANDREW, died on 6 September 1823, probate St Jan, Danish West Indies. [RAK: 1807-1826, FO.107/8]

BULLION, ..., a Captain of Mackay's Regiment, in Danish service 1626, in Swedish service 1629. [TGSI.VIII.187]

BUNTIN, JASPER, probate 11 April 1770 Christiansted, Danish West Indies. [RAK: IV.4]

BUNTON, RICHARD, probate 7 April 1781 Fredericksted, Danish West Indies. [RAK]

BURNET, J., a soldier of the 1st Company of Cockburn's Regiment in Swedish service, 1609. [SIS#217]

CABEL, JAMES, born 1779, died in St Thomas, Danish West Indies, on 6 July 1816. [Dundee Howff g/s]

CAITHNESS, ELIZABETH, or VOLKMAN, in Norway, daughter of Charles Caithness a shipmaster in Dundee, 1831. [NAS.SH.1831]

CAITHNESS, MARGARET, or ULICH, in Norway, daughter of Charles Caithness a shipmaster in Dundee, 1831. [NAS.SH.1831]

CAITHNESS, MARY, in Ask, Norway, daughter of Charles Caithness a shipmaster in Dundee, 1831. [NAS.SH.1831]

CALDWELL, JAMES ALEXANDER, died on 27 July 1766, probate Christiansted, Danish West Indies. [RAK: 1761-1768, fo.262]

CALHOUN, Dr DAVID, probate 8 September 1779 Christiansted, Danish West Indies. [RAK: CCC..XIV.126]

CALHOUN, Captain WILLIAM, 'dead on the coast of Guinea', probate 22 July 1760 Christiansted, Danish West Indies. [RAK]

CAMPBELL, ALEXANDER, authorised to recruit 300 men for service in Sweden, 1573. [NAS.PC1.7.71]

CAMPBELL, ALEXANDER, a soldier of the 1st Company of Cockburn's Regiment in Swedish service, 1609. [SIS#17]

CAMPBELL, ALEXANDER, a surgeon in St Croix, Danish West Indies, testament confirmed with the Commissariat of Edinburgh on 21 September 1782. [NAS]

CAMPBELL, ANN, wife of James McNeilledge in St Croix, Danish West Indies, died in New York on 24 August 1803. [DPCA#66]

CAMPBELL, ARCHIBALD, husband of Tabitha J. Downing, probate 3 July 1769 Christiansted, Danish West Indies. [RAK]

CAMPBELL, COLIN, born in Edinburgh on 1 July 1686, son of John Campbell and his wife Margaret Stewart, founder of the Swedish East India Company in 1731, *Ministre Plenipotentiare* to the Emperor of China, the Great Mogul, etc., married Elizabeth Clarges, died in Gothenburg, Sweden, on 9 May 1757. [NS.7.1.145][AUR.42.38][SBL.VII. 264][SIS#58]

CAMPBELL, HUGH, son of John Campbell and Margaret Stewart, co-director of the Swedish East India Company in 1730s. [SE#117]

CAMPBELL, JARRETT, AND DOBSON, merchants in Stockholm, Sweden, in 1718. [NAS.GD158.1623]

CAMPBELL, JOHN, a merchant in St Croix, Danish West Indies, then in Greenock, testament confirmed with the Commissariat of Glasgow on 7 April 1769. [NAS]

CAMPBELL, JOHN, probate 3 November 1779 Christiansted, Danish West Indies. [RAK: C.III.313]

CAMPBELL, JOHN, probate 16 August 1780 Christiansted, Danish West Indies. [RAK: CCC.XXXV.189]

CAMPBELL, ROBERT, a merchant in Stockholm, Sweden, 1724. [NAS.RS.Dunbarton#5/130]

CAMPBELL, WILLIAM, a Jacobite, Captain of Ogilvy's Regiment in 1746, settled in Gothenburg, Sweden, by 1747. [SHR.lxx.63]

CAMPBELL, ..., in Swedish Service, died in Skara, West Gotland, Sweden, on 2 July 1571. [NAS.GD149.266.169]

CARLE, PATRICK, in Pittochie, Aberdeenshire, a recruit for
Danish service, 1627. [HG.III.407]

CARLYLE, JOHN, probate 30 August 1767 Christiansted, Danish
West Indies. [RAK: XXXX.VII.]

CARMANNO, ALEXANDER, traveller in Denmark, in Skaelskor
by 1610, son of William Carmanno and his wife Christine
Baad. [Dundee birthbrief, CBIII]

CARMANNO, ROBERT, traveller in Denmark, in Skaelskor by
1610, son of William Carmanno and his wife Christine Baad.
[Dundee birthbrief, CBIII]

CARMICHAEL, ALEXANDER, a surgeon in St Croix, Danish
West Indies, possibly from Greenock, testament confirmed
with the Commissariat of Edinburgh on 21 September 1782.
[NAS.CC8.8.125.2]

CARMICHAEL, ...Captain of Mackay's Regiment, in Danish
service 1626, in Swedish service 1629, killed at Bredenburg.
[TGSI.VIII.186]

CARMICK, JAMES, probate 22 May 1767 Christiansted, Danish
West Indies. [RAK]

CARNEGIE, DAVID, a Jacobite Cavalry officer, a refugee in
Sweden in 1746. [GK#111][SHR...63]

CARNEGIE, DAVID, born 1772, son of George Carnegie and
Susan Scott, to Gothenburg, Sweden, in 1786, a merchant
there, made a burgher in 1801, died there in 1873.
[SE#118][SIS#64]

CARNEGIE, DAVID, born 1813, to Sweden in 1830, a merchant
then a sugar refiner and brewer, returned to Scotland in
1841. [SE#121]

CARNEGIE, GEORGE, born 18 November 1726, son of Sir John
Carnegie of Pittarrow, Angus, and his wife Mary Burnett, an
apprentice merchant in Montrose, a Jacobite in 1745,
escaped via Montrose to Gothenburg, Sweden, in 1746, a

merchant there, returned to Scotland in 1765, died in 1786.
[GK#111][NS.7.1.23/145][LPR#320][NS.11.1][SHR.lxx.63]
[Goteborgs Landarkivet,1755][SE#117][SIS#53]

CARNEGIE, JAMES, of Balnamoon, Menmuir, Angus, born 1713, eldest son of Alexander Carnegie, Jacobite Captain of Ogilvy's Regiment in 1745, escaped via Montrose to Gothenburg, Sweden, in 1746, a book-keeper in Gothenburg during 1760s, partner in the merchant house of Carnegy and Shepherd in Gothenburg 1771-1779, died in Scotland 1791. [P.2.100][OR#2][GK#111][AUL.MS2937.3.4][SHR.lxx.63] [Goteborgs Landsarkivet, 1771][SE#117][SIS#63]

CARNEGIE, JOHN or HANS, a merchant in Gothenburg, Sweden, around 1630. [SE#112][SIS#63]

CARWAL, JAMES ALEXANDER, probate 29 May 1767 Christiansted, Danish West Indies. [RAK]

CATLOW, ALEXANDER, husband of Mary ...., probate 10 May 1747 St Croix, Danish West Indies. [RAK]

CHALMERS, Sir WILLIAM, travelled with the Swedish East India Company to China in the 1740s, later a horticulturalist at Kew Gardens, London. [SIS#61]

CHALMERS, WILLIAM, a merchant in Gothenburg, Sweden, around 1750. [Goteborgs Landarkivet]

CHALMERS, WILLIAM, jr, a director of the Swedish East India Company, founder of the Sahlgren Hospital in Gothenburg, Sweden, and of the Chalmers Institute of Technology, died in 1811. [SE#119]

CHARTERS, ALEXANDER, a merchant from Edinburgh, applied to be a burgess of Bergen, Norway, in 1739. [SAB]

CHISHOLM, Captain HUMPHREY, probate 24 March 1779 Christiansted, Danish West Indies. [RAK: CCC.XXXXVIII.198]

CHRISTIANSEN, CHRISTIAN FREDRICH, born 1791 in Copenhagen, Denmark, arrived in Leith on 24 June 1811, resident there. [ECA.SL115.2.2/67]

CHRISTIANSON, THOMAS, from Germiston, Orkney, a burgess of Bergen, Norway, in 1615. [POAS.XIII.39]

CHRISTIE, ANDREW DAVIDSON, (Anders Davidssen Krysted), from Montrose, Angus, a burgess of Bergen, Norway, in 1654. [SAB]

CHRISTIE, JAMES, son of John Christie from Arbroath, a merchant in Gothenburg, Sweden, during 1790s, died in 1806. [SE#119]

CHRISTIE, JOHN, from Arbroath, Angus, a merchant in Gothenburg, Sweden, by 1799. [NS#7/1/31]

CHRISTISON, DAVID, a merchant in Bergen, Norway, in 1696, 1699. [NAS.RD4.79.576; RD3.92.240]

CLAPPERTON, SAMUEL SPENCE, born 1576 in Coldstream, Berwickshire, son of Reverend John Clapperton and his wife Joanna Spence, a Colonel of Horse under Gustavus Adolphus, late Governor of Finland, died in Womar during 1622. [F.2.40]

CLARK, JAMES, (Jakob Clerck), a shipbuilder in Sweden around 1607.[SIS#52]

CLAUSEN, LEENART, harpooner on the whaling ship City of Aberdeen of Aberdeen to Greenland in 1754. [NAS.E508.51.8]

CLEGHORN, ADAM, probate 11 October 1736, St Thomas, Danish West Indies. [RAK]

CLEGHORN, JAMES, a merchant in Gothenburg, Sweden, in 1766. [NAS.RS27.173.132; 186.154]

CLERK, JAMES, (Jakob Clerck), a goldsmith in Stockholm, Sweden, around 1610. [SIS#54]

CLERK, JOHN, (Johan Klerck), was buried in St Peter's, Malmo, Sweden, in 1610. [SAM]

CLERK, R., (Reinhold Klerck), was buried in St Peter's, Malmo, Sweden, on 19 December 1614. [SAM]

CLERK, RICHARD, born in Montrose, Angus, during 1604, a Vice Admiral in the service of Gustavus Adolphus of Sweden. [ANQ.4.320][SHR,IX.269]

CLERK, WILLIAM, to Sweden as a Captain of a Scots Regiment in 1607. [SHR.IX.268]

COATES, MARY ANN, in St Thomas, Danish West Indies, 1866. [NAS.GD1.1079.19]

COCHRANE, FERGUS, born in Kirkcudbright during December 1804, son of Robert Cochran and his wife Elizabeth Guthrie, a merchant in New York by 1830, died in St Croix, Danish West Indies, on 8 December 1831. [ANY.II.135]

COCHRANE, JOHN, a witness in Copenhagen, Denmark, 1649. [NAS.GD84.2.209]

COCHRANE, ROBERT, died 3 April 1755, probate St Croix, Danish West Indies. [RAK: 1751-1766, fo.129]

COCKBURN, SAMUEL, born around 1574, Captain of Foot in Swedish service in Livonia in 1606, fought in Russia 1610, Major General of the Swedish Army, settled in Finland 1616-1621, wounded near Riga and died there during December 1621, and was buried in Abo Minster in Finland. [SIS#30] [CFR#253]

COLLIE, MARGARET, from Kincardine, married David Cunningham, settled in Copenhagen, Denmark, before 1591. [MSC.II.12]

COLLINS, LUCAS, son of Thomas Collins in St Croix, Danish West Indies, apprenticed to John McKinlay a merchant in Edinburgh on 17 October 1799. [Register of Apprentices in Edinburgh]

COLLINS, MARGARET MOTH, daughter of Thomas Collins in St Croix, Danish West Indies, married Thomas Vaughan a painter in Edinburgh, in Canongate, Edinburgh, on 22 December 1797. [Canongate Marriage Register]

COLLINS, MARGARET, daughter of Thomas Collins in St Croix, Danish West Indies, married Ebenezer Prentice a merchant in Glasgow, there on 18 August 1801. [SM#63/587]

COLQUHOUN or CAHUN, JOHN, an army officer in Sweden by 1560s, fought at the battle of Axtorna in 1565. [SIS#21]

COLT, ALEXANDER, son of David Colt and his wife Marjory Irving in Fingask, Daviot, Aberdeenshire, settled in Elsinore, Denmark, during 1587. [MSC.II.31]

CONSTABLE, JACOB, in St Croix, Danish West Indies, 1790. [Caribbeana#5/265]

CONSTABLE, W., a soldier of the 2nd Company of Cockburn's Regiment in Swedish service during 1609. [SIS#217]

COOPER, ANN, youngest daughter of Arthur Cooper, died in St Croix, Danish West Indies, on 2 September 1802. [EA#4053/02]

COOPER, ELIZABETH, daughter of Arthur Cooper in St Croix, Danish West Indies, married Charles Wighton from Tobago in Canongate Church, Edinburgh, on 19 April 1800. [GC#1356][AJ#2730][Canongate Parish Register]

COOPER, GEORGE, in St Croix, Danish West Indies, 1821; died in Edinburgh on 16 January 1822. [NAS.RD5.204.550][DPCA#1017][AJ#3864]

COOPER, HENRY, a merchant in St Croix, Danish West Indies, 1795, husband of Henrietta sometime in St Kitts then in Inverness. [NAS.GD23.5.353]

COOPER, MARGARET, daughter of Arthur Cooper in 'Santa Cruz', married Dr Charles Kennedy, a physician in 'Santa Cruz', in Eyemouth, Berwickshire, during October 1797. [EEC#392]

CORNELIUSEN, SYMON, harpooner on the whaling ship Dundee of Dundee to Greenland in 1753 and in 1754. [NAS.E508.51.8]

CORRIE, JOSEPH, a merchant in St Thomas, Danish West Indies, 1783. [NAS.SH.1783]

COWIE, JAMES, son of William Cowie, formerly an indweller of Leith, settled in Bergen, Norway, by 1579. [ECA.Moses.270/8461]

CRAIG, FRANCIS, from 'Burke', a burgess of Bergen, Norway, in 1647. [SAB]

CRAIGIE, Captain WILLIAM, husband of Anna ...., probate 26 February 1773 Fredericksted, Danish West Indies. [RAK]

CRAWFORD, JAMES, probate 30 June 1779 Christiansted, Danish West Indies. [RAK: CCCL.XXII.268]

CRAWFORD, JAMES, in Copenhagen, Denmark, 1796. [NAS.NRAS.3955.60.1.58]

CRAWFORD, MARGARET, married George Steineth Harding, from St Croix, Danish West Indies, in Fairfield, Ayrshire, on 26 August 1811. [DPCA#476]; Margaret Crawford, wife of George S. Harding, died in St Croix during October 1835. [Logie g/s, Stirling]

CROMARTY, THOMAS, a merchant burgess in Bergen, Norway, by 1639, formerly in Walls, Orkney. [NAS.RS43.6.67; GD195.49]

CROMARTY, WILLIAM, in Bergen, Norway, son of Thomas Cromarty in Kirkbister, Orkney, 1631. [NAS.RS43.4.277]

CROZIER, WILLIAM, probate 3 July 1769 Christiansted, Danish West Indies. [RAK]

CUMLAQUOY, JAMES, from Orkney, in Norway 1632. [NAS.RS43.4.292]

CUNNINGHAM, A., an assistant ensign of Cockburn's Regiment in Swedish service, 1609. [SIS#216]

CUNNINGHAM, JAMES, probate 31 October 1768 Fredericksted, Danish West Indies. [RAK]

CUNNINGHAM, JOHN, born 1575 in Fife, appointed a Captain of the Danish Navy in 1603, led an expedition from Copenhagen to Greenland in 1605, and another to Labrador and Greenland in 1606, in 1619 he was appointed Governor of Vardohuus in northern Norway, died in 1651. [DCB.I.243]

CUNNINGHAM, JOHN, probate 1745 St Croix, Danish West Indies. [RAK]

CUNNINGHAM, THOMAS, from Crail, Fife, a grocer in Stockholm, Sweden, drowned in 1697, buried in Riddarholms Church. [SHR.XXV.292]

CUNNINGHAM, WILLIAM, died on 8 December 1768, probate St Jan, Danish West Indies. [RAK: 1758-1775, fo.64-67]

CURRIE, DAVID, from Newlaw, died in St Thomas, Danish West Indies, on 28 February 1782. [SM#44/221]

CURSITER, or QUOYBANKS, THOMAS, from Orkney, a cooper in Bergen, Norway, 1634. [NAS.RS43.5.39]

DAHL, AMUND, master of the Saint Ann of Lerwick, arrived in Dundee on 14 June 1729 from Langesund, Norway. [NAS.E70.1.1]

DANIELSON, JOHN, from Orkney, admitted as a burgess of Bergen, Norway, in 1626. [SAB]

DAVIDSON, ALEXANDER, from Scotland, a burgess of Bergen, Norway, in 1632. [SAB]

DAVIDSON, ANDREW, from Orkney, admitted as a burgess of Bergen, Norway, in 1619. [SAB][POAS.xii.39]

DAVIDSON, CHARLES, probate 12 May 1779 Christiansted, Danish West Indies. [RAK: CCCL.XXXI.278]

DAVIDSON, FRANCIS, from Orkney, admitted as a burgess of Bergen, Norway, in 1630. [SAB]

DAVIDSON, GEORGE, from Kirkcaldy, Fife, a burgess of Bergen, Norway, in 1631. [SAB]

DAVIDSON, JAMES, from Edinburgh, a burgess of Bergen, Norway, in 1614. [SAB]

DAVIDSON, WILLIAM, a cooper from Orkney, admitted as a burgess of Bergen, Norway, in 1628. [SAB]

DAVIDSON, WILLIAM, (Willumb Dauidssen), from Dysart, Fife, a burgess of Bergen, Norway, in 1631. [SAB]

DAWLING, JAMES, a shipmaster from South Queensferry, master of the Anna of Inverness, died in Stockholm, Sweden, in May 1720. [NAS.AC9.702]

DENOON, ..., an Ensign of Mackay's Regiment in Swedish service from 1629, promoted in Ruthven's Regiment. [TGSI.VIII.188]

DEUCHAR, ANDREW, master of the Catherina of Gothenburg, testament confirmed with the Commissariat of Edinburgh on 16 June 1763. [NAS]

DICK, WILLIAM, a Lieutenant Colonel in Swedish service, in Copenhagen, Denmark, 1649. [NAS.GD84.2.209]

DICKSON, JAMES, born in Montrose, Angus, during 1784, son of James Dickson (1748-1826) a merchant there, emigrated to Sweden in 1809, a merchant in Gothenburg, died 1865. [NS.7/1/24][SE#120][SIS#69]

DICKSON, JOHN, from Orkney, admitted as a burgess of Bergen, Norway, in 1642. [SAB]

DICKSON, ROBERT, born in Montrose, Angus, during 1782, son of James Dickson (1748-1826) a merchant there, emigrated to Sweden in 1802, a merchant in Gothenburg, died 1858. [NS.7/1/24][SE#120][SIS#69]

DISHINGTON, Captain JACOB, died 9 May 1776, probate Christiansted, Danish West Indies. [RAK: 1773-1777, fo.216]

DONNEL, JAMES, probate 6 December 1780 Christiansted, Danish West Indies. [RAK: CCCC.XLI]

DOUGLAS, JAMES, probate 12 November 1776 Fredericksted, Danish West Indies. [RAK: fo.177]

DOUGLAS, ROBERT, a soldier of the 1st Company of Cockburn's Regiment in Swedish service, 1609. [SIS#207]

DOUGLAS, ROBERT, born 1611, to Sweden in 1627, General of the Swedish Army in Germany, and son of Patrick Douglas of Standingstone, Lothian, and his wife Christina Lessels; settled in Stjarnorp, Ostergotland, Sweden, died in Stockholm, during 1661. [RGS.IX.1995][SIS#47]

DOWNIE, JOHN JOHNSON, from St Andrews, Fife, admitted as a burgess of Bergen, Norway, in 1625. [SAB]

DRUMMOND, ALEXANDER, a soldier of the 2nd Company of Cockburn's Regiment in Swedish service, 1609. [SIS#217]

DRUMMOND, DAVID, born 1593, a Lieutenant of the Swedish Life Guards in 1617, enobled in Sweden in 1627, Commander of the Smaland Regiment in 1627, in Stettin, Pomerania, 1631-1634, Major General of the Swedish Army by 1634, died a prisoner in Spandau during 1638, buried in Stockholm. [SIS#42]

DRUMMOND, JOHN, from Edinburgh, Ensign of a Regiment in Swedish service, shipped from Leith via Cromarty to Stralsund, Germany, in 1638. [RPCS.VII.84]

DRUMMOND, Captain JOHN, settled in Sweden by 1723. [PRO.SP54.13.116]

DRUMMOND, WILLIAM, son of Sir John Drummond of Machany, Perthshire, and his wife Margaret Stewart, a Lieutenant of the French Royal Ecossais, Jacobite in 1746, settled in Gothenburg, Sweden, by 1747. [SHR.lxx.63]

DRYDEN, JAMES, a shipmaster from Fisherrow near Edinburgh, a burgess of Bergen, Norway, in 1692. [SAB]

DUMBRECK, CHRISTIAN, second daughter of William Dumbreck in South Coates, Edinburgh, married William Ruan MD at Hannah's Rest, Estate, St Croix, Danish West Indies, on 16 February 1823. [BM#15/492][MUG#249]

DUNBAR, JAMES, a Major of Mackay's Regiment in Danish service 1626, in Swedish service 1629, killed at Bredenburg. [TGSI.VIII.187]

DUNBAR, ..., a Lieutenant of Mackay's Regiment in Danish service 1626, in Swedish service 1629, promoted in Ruthven's Regiment. [TGSI.VIII.187]

DUNBAR, PATRICK, an Ensign of Mackay's Regiment, in Swedish service 1629, wounded at Stralsund. [TGSI.VIII.188]

DUNCANSON, BERNT, from Orkney, admitted as a burgess of Bergen, Norway, in 1635. [SAB]

DUNDEE, BLASIUS, born pre 1550, settled in Sweden in 1576, a banker and burgher of Stockholm from 1583, died in 1621. [SIS#25]

DUNLOP, ANNA, daughter of John Dunlop in St Croix, Danish West Indies, married John Edgar, a surgeon in Ayr, in Irvine, Ayrshire, on 9 November 1821. [AJ#3854]

DUNLOP, JOHN, a merchant in St Croix, Danish West Indies, co-owner of the Peggy, 236 tons, in 1784, [Greenock Ship Register]; in St Croix 1790. [Caribbeana#5/265]; died in St Croix on 25 July 1805. [GM#75/881]

DURIE, CHARLES, HM Consul in Christianna, Norway, son of John Durie a merchant in Dunfermline, Fife, 1830. [NAS.SH.1830]

EFFUARTSON, MAGNUS, from Orkney, a burgess of Bergen, Norway, in 1644. [SAB]

EFFUARTSON, THOMAS, from Orkney, a burgess of Bergen, Norway, in 1632. [SAB]

ELPHINSTONE, H., Captain of the 1st Company of Cockburn's Regiment in Swedish service, 1609. [SIS#216]

ERSKINE, THOMAS, born around 1745, fifth son of David Erskine, a merchant in Gothenburg, Sweden, during 1760s, founder of the Royal Bachelors Club in 1769, married Anne Gordon in Gothenburg in 1771, appointed British consul in Gothenburg from 1775, there 1791, returned to Scotland around 1800, appointed a Knight Commander of the Order of Gustavus Adolphus in 1808, died in Cambo, Fife, in 1828. [SE#117][SIS#63/65] [NAS.GD51.6.916][SP.V.94]

EWARTSON, JOHN, from Orkney, a burgess of Bergen, Orkney, in 1621. [SAB]

EWARTSON, MAGNUS, from Orkney, a burgess of Bergen, Norway, 1621. [POAS.XII.39][SAB]

FARQUHAR, WILLIAM, in Bergen, Norway, 1767. [NAS.GD427.198]

FEA, MARCUS, a cooper from Orkney, a burgess of Bergen, Norway, in 1642. [SAB]

FIELDS, JAMES and SARAH, probate 17 September 1760 Christiansted, Danish West Indies. [RAK]

FINLAY, THOMAS, in St Croix, Danish West Indies, 1790. [Caribbeana#5/265]

FINLAYSON, JAMES, a soldier of the 1st Company of Cockburn's Regiment in Swedish service, 1609. [SIS#217]

FINNIESON, PETER WILLIAMSON, from Scotland, admitted as a burgess of Bergen, Norway, in 1624. [SAB]

FLETCHER, GEORGE, a merchant in Gothenburg, Sweden, trading with Scotland around 1775. [Goteborgs Landsarkivet]; died in Dalkeith on 9 June 1775. [SM.37.342]

FLETCHER, ROBERT, from Ballinshoe, Angus, a Jacobite, Major of Ogilvy's Regiment in 1746, escaped on the ...... of North Ferry of Dundee, Captain James Wemyss, from Lunan Bay, Montrose, and landed in Bergen, Morway, on 13 May 1746, settled in Gothenburg, Sweden, by 1747. [SHR.lxx.64][CM#3997]

FLETT, JAMES, (Jacob Flech), a tablemaker from Orkney, a burgess of Bergen, Norway, in 1672. [SAB]

FORATH, Captain ALEXANDER, born in Dundee, an officer of the Swedish Navy from 1611-1627, in Nygranden, Stockholm, Sweden, 1618, killed in 1627. [NAS.GD334.114/116][SIS#52]

FORATH, HANS, born in Dundee, an officer of the Swedish Navy from 1610 to 1628, [SIS#52]

FORBES, ALEXANDER, Master of Forbes, a Colonel in Swedish service, 1631-1635. [NAS.GD52.93/95]

FORBES, Lord ALEXANDER, testament subscribed in Stockholm, Sweden, on 6 April 1672. [NAS.GD52.1159]

FORBES, DAVID JOHNSON, from Aberdeen, admitted as a burgess of Bergen, Norway, in 1625. [SAB]

FORBES, DUNCAN, Captain of Mackay's Regiment in Danish service, 1626, in Swedish service 1629, killed at Bredenburg. [TGSI.VIII.186]

FORBES, HENRY of Tolquon, a soldier in Swedish service, died at Kirkholm, Russia, in 1605. [SIS#49]

FORBES, JAMES, a planter in St Croix, Danish West Indies, then in the Old Manse of Glass, testament confirmed on on 20 March 1810 and on 22 August 1821 with the Commissariat of Moray. [NAS.CC16.4.9.469; CC16.9.10.271]

FORBES, JOHN, born around 1570, a Calvinist theologian who was exiled by James VI, in Sweden from 1608 to 1610. [SIS#49]

FORBES, JOHN, of Tullich, a Major of Mackay's Regiment in Danish service 1626, in Swedish service 1629, killed at Nordlingen during 1634. [TGSI.VIII.185]

FORBES, PETER, (Petter Forbos), a burgher of Ny Lodose, Sweden, by the 1590s. [SIS#24]

FORBES, WILLIAM, chaplain of Mackay's Regiment, in Danish service 1626, in Swedish service 1629. [TGSI.VIII.189]

FORBES, WILLIAM, a merchant from Aberdeen, applied to become a burgess of Bergen, Norway, in 1706. [SAB]

FORREST, ELIZABETH, only child of Robert Forrest a shipmaster in St Croix, Danish West Indies, testament confirmed on 28 April 1774 with the Commissariat of Edinburgh. [NAS.CC8.8]

FORREST, JAMES, a merchant in Stockholm, was admitted as a burgess and guildsbrother of Ayr on 7 September 1709. [ABR]

FORREST, ROBERT, a merchant in Stockholm, was admitted as a burgess and guildsbrother of Ayr on 18 June 1698. [ABR]

FORSANDER, ANDERS, born in Sweden during 1761, from Gothenburg to Leith in 1782, servant to Douglas of Garold, residing in Greenend near Dalkeith in 1798. [ECA.SL115/2/1/110]

FOSS, TOERUFF, arrived in Dundee from Norway in October 1800 'to be instructed in the English language', returned to Norway on 20 June 1801 aboard the Comet of Christiansand, master Peter Nolit. [NAS.CE70.1.9]

FOTHERINGHAM, DAVID, a merchant in Dundee, then Jacobite Governor of Dundee in 1745, escaped on the ..... of North Ferry of Dundee , Captain James Wemyss, from Lunan Bay, Montrose, to Norway, landed in Bergen, on 13 May 1746, later moved to Gothenburg, Sweden. [OR#127][GK#111][SHR.lxx.64][CM#3997]

FOTHERINGHAM, THOMAS, of Ballindean, Dundee, Jacobite of Prince Charles Edward Stuart's Guard in 1746, settled in Gothenburg, Sweden, by 1747. [SHR.lxx.64]

FRASER, ALEXANDER, probate 30 April 1770 Christiansted, Danish West Indies [RAK: CC.V.65]

FRASER, CHARLES, a Jacobite in 1745, Lieutenant Colonel of Fraser's Regiment , settled in Gothenburg, Sweden, by 1747. [SHR.lxx.64]

FRASER, DANIEL, born 5 November 1786 at Ancrum, Roxburghshire, son of Alexander Fraser a carpenter and millwright, settled in Sweden around 1822, an engineer, died 1849. [SHR.xxv.299]

FRASER, EDWARD, a merchant from Glasgow, died in St Croix, Danish West Indies, during September 1802. [EA#4074/03][AJ#2872]

FRASER, HUGH, probate 30 April 1770 Christiansted, Danish West Indies. [RAK: CC.V.65]

FRASER, JAMES, in St Croix, Danish West Indies, around 1790. [Caribbeana#5/265]

FRASER, JOHN, a burgess of Bergen, Norway, husband of Violet Louttit, 1625. [NAS.RS43.III.219]

FRASER, JOHN, a merchant burgess of Altona, Denmark, 1774. [NAS.SC12.6.1744/1]

FRASER, Mr JOHN, in St Croix, Danish West Indies, 1790. [Caribbeana#5/265]

FRASER, W., a soldier of the 2nd Company of Cockburn's Regiment in Swedish service, 1609. [SIS#217]

FREDERICKSEN, FREDERICK, born in Norway, a burgess of Dundee, Scotland, by August 1764 and proprietor of the Mary of Gardenstone. [NAS.CE70.1.4]

FREDERICKSON, MEILIS, burgess of Marstrand, Sweden, 1668. [NAS.NRAS.0336.DB2/bundle29]

FULLARTON, ARCHIBALD, a Lieutenant of Militia in St Croix, Danish West Indies, 1790. [Caribbeana#5/265]

FYFFE, DAVID, (David Feif), second son of Alexander Fyffe a merchant in Montrose, emigrated to Sweden in the 1630s, a draper and burgher of Stockholm. [SIS#55]

FYFFE, DONALD(?), (Donat Feif), youngest son of Alexander Fyffe a merchant in Montrose, emigrated to Sweden in the 1630s, a silk-mercer and burgher of Stockholm. [SIS#55]

FYFFE, JAMES, (Jakob Feif), eldest son of Alexander Fyffe a merchant in Montrose, emigrated to Sweden in 1630s, a brewer and burgher of Stockholm. [SIS#55]

FYFFE, JOHN, (Hans Feiff), a merchant burgher of Gothenburg, Sweden, around 1630. [SE#112]

FYFFE, ROBERT, from Dundee, a burgess of Bergen, Norway, 1631, dead by 1642. [SAB]

GABRIELSON, WILLIAM, from Orkney, a burgess of Bergen, Norway, in 1645. [SAB]

GALBRAITH, ARCHIBALD, died in St Thomas, Danish West Indies, on 1 March 1826. [BM#19/765]

GARDEN, ALEXANDER, of Troup, a Major in Swedish service and Commandant of Brix, 1635-1653. [NAS.GD57.336.1-11]

GARDINER, G., a soldier of the 2nd Company of Cockburn's Regiment in Swedish service, 1609. [SIS#217]

GARDNER, WILLIAM, died in Gothenburg during 1812. [SM.74.806]

GARDYNE, DAVID, from Middleton, Angus, a Jacobite in 1745, Captain of Ogilvy's Regiment, settled in Gothenburg, Sweden, by 1747. [SHR.lxx.64]

GARRIOCH, HENRY, a burgess of Bergen, Norway, 1625.
[NAS.RS43.3.51]

GEORGE, ELIZABETH, wife of William Cunningham, died on 27
February 1768, probate St Jan, Danish West Indies.
[RAK:1749-1770, fo.356]

GEORGESON, ADAM, from Orkney, a burgess of Bergen,
Norway, in 1619. [SAB]

GEORGESON, GEORGE, (Jorgenn Jorgensen), from Dundee,
admitted as a burgess of Bergen, Norway, in 1615. [SAB]

GEORGESON, GEORGE, (Jorgen Jorgensen), from Scotland,
admitted as a burgess of Bergen, Norway, in 1622. [SAB]

GEORGESON, GEORGE, from Old Aberdeen, a burgess of
Bergen, Norway, in 1632. [SAB]

GEORGESON, GILBERT, from Fraserburgh, Aberdeenshire, a
burgess of Bergen, Norway, in 1618. [SAB]

GEORGESON, JAMES, from Dundee, admitted as a burgess of
Bergen, Norway, in 1615. [SAB]

GEORGESON, JOHN, from Aberdeen, admitted as a burgess of
Bergen, Norway, in 1628. [SAB]

GEORGESON, JOHN, from Orkney, a burgess of Bergen,
Norway, in 1643. [SAB]

GIBB, CHARLEY, probate 1769 Christiansted, Danish West
Indies. [RAK:L.XXX.192]

GIBB, JAMES, born 1813, eldest son of John James Gibb a
merchant in Glasgow, died on St Thomas, Danish West
Indies, on 10 May 1832. [ST.VII.490]

GIBSON, WILLIAM, a merchant on St Thomas, Danish West
Indies, died on 14 June 1841, testament was confirmed in
1842. [NAS.SC70.1.61]

GIBSON, WILLIAM, born in Arbroath, Angus, during 1783, son of William Gibson a sail and rope-maker, settled in Gothenburg, Sweden, around 1797, a merchant there, a textile manufacturer and machine maker in Jonsered, Sweden, died 1857. [NS#7/1/24][SE#120][SIS#70]

GIFFARD, B., a soldier of the 3rd Company of Cockburn's Regiment in Swedish service, 1609. [SIS#217]

GILBERT, THOMAS, a soldier of the 2nd Company of Cockburn's Regiment in Swedish service, 1609. [SIS#217]

GILBERTSON, HENRY, (Henrich Gilvertzenn), from 'Cordin', admitted as a burgess of Bergen, Norway, in 1619. [SAB]

GILBERTSON, JOHN, from Scotland, admitted as a burgess of Bergen, Norway, in 1627. [SAB]

GILBERTSON, LAURENCE, from Orkney, a burgess of Bergen, Norway, in 1640. [SAB]

GILBERTSON, THOMAS, from Dornoch (?) (Dornau), applied to become a burgess of Bergen, Norway, in 1642. [SAB]

GILLESPIE, DAVID, son of David Gillespie of Auchlech, Aberdeenshire, and his wife Isobel Watt, emigrated to Denmark by 1589. [MSC.II.7]

GILLESPIE, JOHN, probate 1768 Christiansted, Danish West Indies. [RAK: L.VII.139]

GILMORE, THOMAS, a merchant in Gothenburg, Sweden, 1639. [NAS.B9.12.7.66]

GILROY, ROBERT, a merchant in Christiansund, Norway, admitted as a burgess of Montrose, Angus, in 1788. [Montrose Burgess Roll]

GLASS, WILLIAM, in St Croix, Danish West Indies, around 1784, son of Reverend Hugh Glass and his wife Elizabeth Arnot in Kettle parish, Fife. [NAS.RD3.244.530]

GORDON, Captain ADAM, in Danish service, 1627
[RPCS.15.6.1627][HG.III.407]

GORDON, ADAM, born 1611, Captain of Monro's Regiment in
Swedish service, from Cromarty to Hamburg in 1631, killed
at the Battle of Nordlingen near Munich on 27 August 1634.
[HG.III.408]

GORDON, ADAM, Captain of Mackay's Regiment, in Danish
service 1626, in Swedish service 1629. [TGSI.VIII.186]

GORDON, ALEXANDER, Colonel of the Swedish Army in 1634.
[HG.III.411]

GORDON, ALEXANDER, eldest son of Sir Alexander Gordon of
Navidale, Captain of Cunninghame's Regiment in Swedish
service, from Aberdeen to Sweden on 19 October 1637.
[HG.III.411]

GORDON, ALEXANDER, a Jacobite in 1745, settled in
Gothenburg, Sweden, by 1747. [SHR.lxx.64]

GORDON, ALEXANDER, in St Croix, Danish West Indies, by
1790, [Caribbeana#5/265]; there in 1799.
[NAS.RD3.310.761]; died there on 24 January 1805,
testament confirmed with the Commissariat of Edinburgh on
26 July 1806. [NAS.CC8.8.136]

GORDON, ARCHIBALD, died on 16 June 1736, husband of
Elizabeth ...., probate St Croix, Danish West Indies.
[RAK:1735-1742,fo.10]

GORDON, COSMO, died in St Croix, Danish West Indies, on 26
August 1827. [AJ#4163]

GORDON, GEORGE, a merchant from Banff, applied to become a
burgess of Bergen, Norway, in 1700. [SAB]

GORDON, Dr GEORGE, son of William Gordon, a burgess of
Banff in 1767, graduated MD from King's College,
Aberdeen, on 18 August 1770, probate 29 January 1772
Christiansted, Danish West Indies. [RAK: C.XXXIX.22]
[KCA#133][Banff Burgess Roll]

GORDON, Dr GEORGE, a planter, died on 27 September 1797, husband of Mary Gordon, probate St Jan, Danish West Indies. [RAK: 1797-1807,fo.2/88]

GORDON, GEORGE, in St Croix, Danish West Indies, 1790. [Caribbeana#5/265]

GORDON, HUGH, an officer of Mackay's Regiment, in Danish service 1626, in Swedish service 1629, wounded at Oldenburg. [TGSI.VIII.188]

GORDON, JOHN, son of John Gordon of Crabston, and his wife Elspeth Keith, settled as a merchant in 'Copperberry', Sweden, granted a birth brief by the Sheriff Clerk of Aberdeen on 16 October 1628. [Aberdeen Sheriff Court, Judicial Enactment]

GORDON, JOHN, a Colonel in Swedish service, 1630. [HG.III.443]

GORDON, JOHN, son of Gilbert Gordon of Neinewen, from Cromarty in 1631 to join the army of Gustavus Adolphus. [HG.III.443]

GORDON, JOHN, to Sweden on 19 October 1637 to join Colonel Alexander Cunninghame's Regiment. [HG.III.444]

GORDON, JOHN, son of William Gordon of Cottoun, Aberdeenshire, a Captain of the Swedish Army, died in Cracow, Poland, around 1664. [Aberdeen Birth Brief, 4 June 1668]

GORDON, JOHN, of Glenbucket, Aberdeenshire, born around 1673, son of John Gordon, Jacobite Colonel in 1745, fled via Norway to Gothenburg, Sweden, by 1747, died in Boulogne-sur-mer, France, in 1750. [SHR.lxx.64]

GORDON, JOHN, in St Croix, Danish West Indies, 1790. [Caribbeana#5/265]

GORDON, JOHN, MD, Royal Danish Physician for the Danish West Indies, died in Bath, England, on 16 February 1807.

[SM.69/159][AJ#30851]; John Gordon, MD, from St Croix, Danish West Indies, died on 30 January 1807, aged 53. [Bath Abbey g/s]

GORDON, JOHN, born around 1740, died in Cane Valley, St Croix, Danish West Indies, on 22 July 1824. [BM#16/734]

GORDON, ROBERT, a drummer in James Ramsay's Regiment in Swedish service, 1631. [HG.III.456]

GORDON, ROBERT MELVILLE, in St Croix, Danish West Indies, 1790. [Caribbeana#5/265]

GORDON, SARAH MAJJOUT, daughter of George Gordon in St Croix, Danish West Indies, married Dr William MacDougall in Edinburgh on 26 June 1792. [Edinburgh Marriage Register]

GORDON, WILLIAM, master mariner aboard the <u>Enhiorningen</u>, master Jens Munk, from Copenhagen on 9 May 1619 bound for Hudson's bay, arrived there on 7 September 1619, died there 6 May 1620. [DCB][HG.III.457]

GORDON, WILLIAM, son of William Gordon of Farskane and his wife Helen Duff, a Jacobite in 1715, fled to Paris in 1716, later a merchant in Norway. [JAB#122]

GORDON, WILLIAM, in St Croix, Danish West Indies, 1790. [Caribbeana#5/265]

GRAEME, ..., an officer of Mackay's Regiment, in Danish service 1626, in Swedish service 1629. [TGSI.VIII.188]

GRAHAM, ALEXANDER, a merchant in Dundee, son of David Graham also a merchant in Dundee, a Jacobite of Prince Charles Edward Stuart's Guard in 1745, escaped on the .....of North Ferry of Dundee, Captain James Wemyss, from Lunan Bay, Montrose, to Norway, landed in Bergen on 13 May 1746, later to Sweden.
[GK#114][SHR.lxx.64][CM#3997]

GRAHAM, ALEXANDER, son of Peter Graham an industrialist, settled in Sweden around 1856 as an electrical engineer. [SHR.XXV.299]

GRAHAM, DAVID, of Duntroon, alias Lord Dundee, a Jacobite in 1745, escaped on the ....of North Ferry of Dundee, Captain James Wemyss, from Lunan Bay, Montrose, to Norway, landed in Bergen on 13 May 1746. [CM#3997]

GRAHAM, DAVID, a merchant in Dundee, a Jacobite in 1745, escaped on the ....of North Ferry of Dundee, Captain James Wemyss, from Lunan Bay, Montrose, to Norway, landed in Bergen on 13 May 1746. [CM#3997]

GRAHAM, GEORGE, a merchant in Copenhagen, Denmark, then a planter in St Croix, Danish West Indies, now in Glasgow, 1798. [HCR.213]; died in Glasgow on 12 June 1798. [AJ#2630]; probate 1800 PCC [PRO.789, Adderley]

GRAHAM, JAMES, Viscount Dundee, son of William Graham and his wife Christian Graham, a Jacobite of Prince Charles Edward Stuart's Life Guard in 1745, settled in Gothenburg, Sweden, by 1747, later a French Army officer, died in Dunkirk, France, during 1759. [SHR.lxx.64]

GRAHAM, PATRICK, son of Peter Graham an industrialist, settled in Sweden around 1856 as an electrical engineer. [SHR.xxv.299]

GRAHAM, ROBERT, merchant of the Pelican of Bergen, 1694. [NAS.RD3.83.103]

GRAHAM, ROBERT, of Garvock, a Jacobite in 1745, a Lieutenant of Prince Charles Edward Stuart's Cavalry, settled in Gothenburg, Sweden, by 1747. [SHR.lxx.64]

GRAHAM, WILLIAM, died on 30 November 1750, husband of Mary ....., probate St Croix, Danish West Indies. [RAK: 1747-1754, fo.320]

GRANGER, WALTER, a merchant in Stockholm, Sweden, 1720. [NAS.AC9.962]

GRANT, ALEXANDER, in St Croix, Danish West Indies, 1790.
[Caribbeana#5/625]

GRANT, ALEXANDER, son of Alexander Grant in St Croix,
Danish West Indies, educated at King's College, Aberdeen,
1795-1800, graduated MA. [KCA#2.379/380]

GRANT, ALEXANDER, in St Croix, Danish West Indies, 1809.
[NAS.GD23.6.459]

GRANT, ANNA FRANCES, daughter of Sir Alexander Grant of
Dalvey, married William Marcus Westerman of Copenhagen,
Denmark, there on 1 May 1851. [W#1217]

GRANT, COLIN, in St Croix, Danish West Indies, 1790.
[Caribbeana#5/265]

GRANT, JAMES, born in Abernethy, Strathspey, late of St
Thomas in the Vale, Jamaica, died in St Croix, Danish West
Indies, on 28 October 1830. [AJ#4351]

GRAY, D., an Ensign of the 1st Company of Cockburn's Regiment
in Swedish service, 1609. [SIS#216]

GRAY, ROBERT, son of Andrew Gray a burgess of Aberdeen and
his wife Annabel Lawson, who died in Jutland, Denmark, in
November 1593. [MSC.II.30]

GRAY, WILLIAM, (Villem Graa), buried in St Peter's, Malmo,
Sweden, 1545. [SAM]

GREIG, ALEXANDER, in Bergen, Norway, 1794.
[NAS.GD51.1.621]

GREIG, DAVID, born 1801 in Kilrenny, Fife, died in Greenland on
10 August 1832. [Boarhills, Fife, g/s]

GREIG, HENRY, a merchant in Gothenburg, Sweden, around
1775, trading with Scotland, died in 1790s. [Goteborgs
Landsarkivet]

GREIG, WALTER, a skipper in Christiansund, Norway, 1696.
[NAS.RD4.78.168; RD4.79.509]

GREIG, WALTER, a shipmaster from Aberdeen, applied to become a burgess of Bergen, Norway, in 1704. [SAB]

GRIMSTON, THOMAS CHRISTIANSON, from Orkney, a burgess of Bergen, Norway, in 1615. [SAB]

GROSSART, JOHN, (Joen Crostert), from Leith, a burgess of Bergen, Norway, in 1663. [SAB]

GUNN, GEORGE, an officer of Mackay's Regiment, in Danish service 1626, in Swedish service 1629, [TGSI.VIII.188]

GUNN, JOHN, a soldier of the 2nd Company of Cockburn's Regiment in Swedish service, 1609. [SIS#217]

GUNN, JOHN, an officer of Mackay's Regiment, in Danish service 1626, in Swedish service 1629. [TGSI.VIII.188]

GUNN, Sir WILLIAM, Captain of Mackay's Regiment, in Danish service 1626, in Swedish service 1629, later Colonel of a Dutch Regiment. [TGSI.viii.186]

GUTHRIE, GEORGE, a noble in Sweden by 1684, son of ..... Guthrie from Montrose, Angus. [NAS.GD188.2.1.4]

GUTHRIE, HENRY, (Henrich Gyttrich), from Montrose, Angus, a burgess of Bergen, Norway, in 1650. [SAB]

GUTHRIE, JOHN, from Scotland, a burgess of Bergen, Norway, 1630. [SAB]

GUTHRIE, NICHOLAS, brother of George above, a painter in Sweden, visited England and Scotland in 1684. [NAS.GD188.2.1.4]

HADDEN, ..., Ensign of Mackay's Regiment, in Swedish service 1629, killed at New Brandenburg 1631. [TGSI.VIII.188]

HAGENSSEN, ANNA, in Norway, widow of Oluff Hagenssen, owner of lands in the parish of Sandsting, Shetland, 1603. [Shetland Archives, D11.190]

HAGGART, CHARLES, St Thomas, Danish West Indies, 1789. [NAS.NRAS.0623.T-MJ, 427.36]

HALCRO, HENRY, a cooper in Bergen, Norway, husband of Ann Nicolsdaughter, son of William Halcro a merchant in Kirkwall, Orkney, 1632. [NAS.RS43.4.413]

HALCRO, WILLIAM, a burgess of Trondheim, Norway, son of Robert Halcro of Cava, Orkney, 1634. [NAS.RS43.5.55]

HALL, Dr JAMES, from Dumfries, died in St Croix, Danish West Indies, on 11 June 1824. [EA]

HALL, JOHN, and Company, merchants in Gothenburg, Sweden, around 1775. [NAS.GD171.22/41/112/182] [Goteborgs Landsarkivet]

HALL, MARGARET, daughter of Alexander Hall and his wife Elspet Fraser in Monymusk, Aberdeenshire, died in Elsinore, Denmark, in August 1677. [APB]

HALLIBURTON, ALEXANDER, in Stockholm, Sweden, 1644. [NAS.GD137.86A]

HALLIDAY, JOHN, (Hans Helleday), from Tullibole Castle, Perthshire, a wine merchant in Sweden during 1630s. [SIS#55]

HALLIDAY, RICHARD, a soldier of the 1st Company of Cockburn's Regiment in Swedish service, 1609. [SIS#217]

HAMILTON, Sir ALEXANDER, of Redhouse, a Colonel in Swedish service, cannon-maker at Urbowe, Sweden, around 1630, returned to Scotland, fought in the Wars of the Covenant, killed by an explosion at Dunglass Castle. [TGSI.VIII.160]

HAMILTON, FRANCIS, (Frantz Homiltun), was buried in St Peter's, Malmo, Sweden, in 1564. [SAM]

HAMILTON, FREDERICK, Standard-bearer to Augustus of Norway, General to the Elector of Brandenburg, 1665. [Edinburgh University, Laing Charters #2589]

HAMILTON, HUGH, son of John Hamilton of Sundrum, Captain of the 96th Regiment in St Croix, Danish West Indies, 1810. [NAS.GD51.6.700]

HAMILTON, JAMES, a merchant from Glasgow, in Jutland, Denmark, around 1670. [RPCS.IV.89]

HAMILTON, JAMES, from Cambuskeith, Ayrshire, settled in St Croix, father of Alexander Hamilton, the American politician, born ....1757(?) [DAB.VIII.171]

HAMILTON, WILLIAM, (Willem Hamilton), settled in Karlstad, Sweden, by 1598. [SIS#23]

HAMILTON, WILLIAM, a Jacobite of Prince Charles Edward Stuart's court, settled in Gothenburg, Sweden, by 1747. [SHR.lxx.64]

HANSEN, BRONCHE, harpooner on the whaling ship Dundee of Dundee, to Greenland in 1753. [NAS.E508.51.8]

HANSEN, CHRISTOPHER, of the Faeroes and Iceland Company of Copenhagen, Denmark, 1640. [NAS.RS44.III.465]

HANSEN, FOLCART, steersman on the whaling ship North Star of Dunbar, to Greenland in 1752. [NAS.E508.49.8]

HANSEN, MATTYES, harpooner on the whaling ship City of Aberdeen of Aberdeen, to Greenland in 1754. [NAS.E508.51.8]

HARDIE, JAMES, husband of Elizabeth Birrell, in Sweden before 1823. [NAS.SH.30.7.1823]

HAY, ALEXANDER, a Captain of Mackay's Regiment, in Danish service 1626, in Swedish service 1629, Lieutenant Colonel of Dragoons in the Swedish Army. [SHR.IX.270][TGSI.VIII.186]

HAY, JOHN, son of Thomas Hay a burgess of Aberdeen and his wife Isobel Low, in Horsens, Jutland, Denmark, by 1591. [APB]

HAY, JOHN, a 'vietoris' in Bergen, Norway, father of Alison, 1625. [NAS.SH.1625]

HAY, ROBERT, (Rubbert Hej), from Dysart, Fife, a burgess of Bergen, Norway, in 1619. [SAB]

HEATLEY, GEORGE, a Captain of Mackay's Regiment, in Danish service 1626, in Swedish service 1629, killed at Oberlin. [TGSI.VIII.186]

HENDERSON, ANDREW, a smith from Orkney, a burgess of Bergen, Norway, in 1646. [SAB]

HENDERSON, JAMES, in St Croix, Danish West Indies, 1790. [Caribbeana#5/265]

HENDERSON, JOHN, from Orkney, a burgess of Bergen, Norway, in 1625. [SAB]

HENDERSON, THOMAS, from Orkney, a burgess of Bergen, Norway, in 1643. [SAB]

HENNY, Dr JOHN, in 'Santa Cruz' (St Croix?), admitted as a burgess of Arbroath, Angus, in 1791. [AA: Arbroath Burgess Roll]

HENRIKSON, HENRIK, master of the <u>Rising Sun of Trontheim</u>, was admitted as a burgess and guildsbrother of Glasgow on 3 November 1716. [GBR]

HENRY, JAMES, probate 28 July 1773, Christiansted, Danish West Indies. [RAK: CL.XXIII.157]

HEPBURN, JOHN, born in Scotland around 1598, a Swedish army officer from 1624 to 1632. [SIS#44]

HERCULESON, ANDREW, from Arbroath, Angus, admitted as a burgess of Bergen, Norway, in 1628. [SAB]

HILL, ADAM, probate October 1767 Christiansted, Danish West Indies. [RAK:XXX.VII]

HILL, Dr JAMES, from Dumfries, settled in St Croix, Danish West Indies, married Arabella daughter of Thomas Sherlock of Garrybritts, in London 1810. [EA#4899/303]; died in St Croix on 11 June 1824. [BM#16/488]

HILL, JOSEPH, probate August 1767 Christiansted, Danish West Indies. [RAK]

HILL, ROBERT, a witness in St Croix, Danish West Indies, in 1819. [NAS, RD5,168,283]; a burgher of St Croix in 1820, [NAS.RD5.251.310]

HOLT, ALEXANDER from Montrose, Angus, a burgess of Bergen, Norway, 1641. [SAB]

HOUSTON, ANDREW, probate 4 July 1772 Christiansted, Danish West Indies. [RAK: XXVI.60]

HUME, ROBERT, a Captain of Mackay's Regiment, in Danish service 1626, in Swedish service 1629. [TGSI.VIII.186]

HUNTER, DAVID, of Burnside, Grange of Monifieth, Angus, Captain of the Jacobite Life Guards in 1745, escaped in 1746 from Dundee to Bergen, Norway, and later in Gothenburg, Sweden, by 1747. [LPR#218][GK#114][OR#127][SHR.lxx.64]

HUNTER, JOHN, (Hans Hunter), buried in St Peter's, Malmo. Sweden, 1544. [SAM]

INGSTER, PETER, a weaver from Orkney, a burgess of Bergen, Norway, in 1638. [SAB]

INNES, JOHN, son of William Innes of Sandside, an officer of Mackay's Regiment, in Danish service 1626, in Swedish service 1629, killed at Stralsund. [TGSI.VIII.188]

INNES, PATRICK, a Captain of Mackay's Regiment, in Danish service 1626, in Swedish service 1629, killed at Nurnberg during 1632. [TGSI.VIII.186]

INNES, ROBERT, a Captain of Mackay's Regiment, in Danish service 1626, in Swedish service 1629. [TGSI.VIII.186]

INNES, ROBERT, born on 14 September 1745, son of Robert Innes the town clerk of Banff and his wife Margaret Gilchrist, settled in Gothenburg, Sweden, as a merchant by 1765, admitted as a burgess of Montrose in 1791, by 1795 a merchant in Newcastle. [Montrose Burgess Roll] [NS#7.1.146]

IRVINE, CHARLES, born in 1693, son of James Irvine of Artamford, Aberdeenshire, and his wife Margaret Sutherland, probably a Jacobite in 1715, settled in France as a merchant in Rouen, later a supercargo of the Swedish East India Company of Gothenburg, died in Aberdeen on 8 October 1771. [AUR.42.43][NS#7.1.146][SE#117]

IRVINE, JOHN, probate 30 September 1770 Fredericksted, Danish West Indies. [RAK: fo.56]

IRVINE, JOHN, in Gothenburg, Sweden, later in Aberdeen, 1792. [NAS.RS8.224]; testament confirmed with the Commissariat of Aberdeen in 1795. [NAS]

IRVINE, LINDSAY, probate 7 April 1781 Fredericksted, Danish West Indies. [RAK: fo.40]

IRVINE, RICHARD, probate 31 May 1769 Christiansted, Danish West Indies. [RAK:XX.33]

IRVINE, THOMAS, born on 30 September 1685, son of James Irvine of Artamford, Aberdeenshire, and his wife Margaret Sutherland, settled in Sweden as a merchant in Gothenburg, enobled there in 1757, married Margaret Irvine, died in Gothenborg on 2 December 1765. [NS#7.1.146][Goteborgs Landsarkivet]

IRVING, ALEXANDER, a burgess of Bergen, Norway, in 1636. [NAS.RS43.5.230]

IRVING, ALEXANDER, from Aberdeenshire, a Lieutenant Colonel in Swedish service, 1642. [NAS.RH16.207.2]

JACOBSON, GILBERT, from Orkney, a burgess of Bergen, Norway, in 1615. [POAS.XIII.39]

JACOBSON, JACOB, from Orkney, a burgess of Bergen, Norway, in 1623. [POAS.XIII.39]

JACOBSON, JOACHIM, from Orkney, a burgess of Bergen, Norway, in 1583. [POAS.XIII.39]

JACOBSON, JOHN, from Shetland, a burgess of Bergen, Norway, in 1612. [POAS.XIII.39]

JACOBSON, MAGNUS, from Orkney, a burgess of Bergen, Norway, in 1612. [POAS.XIII.39]

JACOBSON, ..., from Orkney, a burgess of Bergen, Norway, in 1621. [POAS.XIII.39]

JAMIESON, ANDREW, from St Andrews, Fife, admitted as a burgess of Bergen, Norway, in 1628. [SAB]

JAMIESON, DANIEL, from Scotland, a burgess of Bergen, Norway, in 1614. [SAB]

JAMIESON, GILBERT, from Orkney, a burgess of Bergen, Norway, 1615. [SAB]

JAMIESON, JAMES, from Orkney, a burgess of Bergen, Norway, in 1623. [SAB]

JAMIESON, JOHN, from 'Kennis' in Scotland, a burgess of Bergen, Norway, in 1619. [SAB]

JAMIESON, JOHN, a shipmaster in Elsinore, Denmark, by 1650. [Dundee Archives, CB.III/232]

JAMIESON, MAGNUS, from Orkney, a burgess of Bergen, Norway, in 1621. [SAB]

JAMIESON, RICHARD, from Aberdeen, admitted as a burgess of Bergen, Norway, in 1617. [SAB]

JAMIESON, ROBERT, (Rubbert Jacobsen), from Kirkcaldy, Fife, a burgess of Bergen, Norway, in 1621. [SAB]

JAMIESON, THOMAS, from Moray (?), (Mara), a burgess of Bergen, Norway, in 1632. [SAB]

JAMIESON, THOMAS, from Peterhead, Aberdeenshire, a burgess of Bergen, Norway, in 1634. [SAB]

JAMIESON, THOMAS, from Orkney, a burgess of Bergen, Norway, in 1637. [SAB]

JAMIESON, THOMAS, a cooper from Orkney, a burgess of Bergen, Norway, in 1647. [SAB]

JAMIESON, WALTER, a cooper from Scotland, a burgess of Bergen, Norway, in 1614. [SAB]

JANSEN, ANDREW, harpooner on the whaling ship Prince of Wales of Leith to Greenland in 1753. [NAS.E508.50.8]

JANSEN, DIRCK, harpooner on the whaling ship Campbeltown of Leith to Greenland in 1753. [NAS.E508.50.8/7]

JANSEN, RIEWERT, harpooner on the whaling ship Dundee of Dundee to Greenland 1753. [NAS.E508.51.8]

JENSEN, OLE, a shipmaster in Kreagoire, 1749. [NAS.RD2.167.277/295]

JOHNSON, ANDREW, from Orkney, a burgess of Bergen, Norway, in 1574. [POAS.XIII.39]

JOHNSON, ANDREW, from Orkney, a burgess of Bergen, Norway, in 1614. [POAS.XIII.39]

JOHNSON, ANDREW, a cooper from Aberdeen, a burgess of Bergen, Norway, in 1629. [SAB]

JOHNSON, ANDREW, from Scotland, a burgess of Bergen, Norway, in 1632. [SAB]

JOHNSON, ANDREW, from Orkney, a burgess of Bergen, Norway, in 1636. [SAB]

JOHNSON, CHARLES, (Carl Jensen), a merchant from Berwick, a burgess of Bergen, Norway, in 1695. [SAB]

JOHNSON, CHRISTIAN, from Shetland, a burgess of Bergen, Norway, in 1575. [POAS.XIII.39]

JOHNSON, CHRISTIAN, a burgess of Bergen, Norway, by 1594, son of Merette Williamsdotter in Yell, Shetland. [PSAS.XIV.27-29]

JOHNSON, DAVID, from Fraserburgh (Faridzbroch), Aberdeenshire, applied to become a burgess of Bergen, Norway, in 1641. [SAB]

JOHNSON, HENRY, from Orkney, a burgess of Bergen, Orkney, in 1616. [SAB][POAS.XIII.39]

JOHNSON, JAMES, a cooper from Orkney, a burgess of Bergen, Norway, in 1626. [SAB]

JOHNSON, JOHN, from Orkney, a burgess of Bergen, Norway, in 1615. [SAB][POAS.XIII.39]

JOHNSON, JOHN, a weaver from Orkney, a burgess of Bergen, Norway, in 1619. [SAB][POAS.XIII.39]

JOHNSON, JOHN, from Orkney, a burgess of Bergen, Norway, in 1626. [SAB]

JOHNSON, JOHN, a cooper from Leith, a burgess of Bergen, Norway, in 1636. [SAB]

JOHNSON, MICHAEL, (Michell Joenssen), from Orkney, a burgess of Bergen, Norway, in 1653. [SAB]

JOHNSON, PETER, from Dundee, a burgess of Bergen, Norway, in 1625. [SAB]

JOHNSON, ROBERT, from Aberdeen, a burgess of Bergen, Norway, in 1623. [SAB]

JOHNSON, ROBERT, from Scotland, a burgess of Bergen, Norway, in 1631. [SAB]

JOHNSON, STEVEN, from Orkney, a burgess of Bergen, Orkney, in 1615. [SAB][POAS.XIII.39]

JOHNSON, THOMAS, from Aberdeen, a burgess of Bergen, Norway, in 1614. [SAB]

JOHNSON, THOMAS, a cooper from Quebanks, Orkney, a burgess of Bergen, Norway, in 1618. [SAB][POAS.XIII.39]

JOHNSON, THOMAS, from Anstruther, Fife, was admitted as a burgess of Bergen, Norway, in 1627. [SAB]

JOHNSON, THOMAS, from Dundee, a burgess of Bergen, Norway, in 1632. [SAB]

JOHNSTON, ALEXANDER, a silversmith in Dundee, a Jacobite Life Guard in 1745, escaped from Dundee to Bergen, Norway, in 1746, settled in Gothenburg, Sweden, by 1747, later moved to France. [LPR#218][OR#127][SHR.lxx.64]

JOHNSTON, ANNA, probate 29 June 1774 Christiansted, Danish West Indies. [RAK: CC.VII.80]

JOHNSTON, D., & Company, merchants in Gothenburg, Sweden, during 1770s, trading with Scotland. [Goteborgs Landsarkivet]

JOHNSTON, JAMES, a planter, died on 12 October 1799, probate 1799 St Jan, Danish West Indies. [RAK: 1797-1807, fo.10]

JOHNSTON, WILLIAM, from Orkney, a burgess of Bergen, Norway, in 1576. [POAS.XIII.39]

JOHNSTON, WILLIAM WILLIAMSON, from Dysart, Fife, admitted as a burgess of Bergen, Norway, in 1626. [SAB]

JOHNSTON, WILLIAM, a planter, died on 25 August 1802, husband of Mary Leonard Scatliff, probate St Jan, Danish West Indies. [RAK: 1797-1807, fo.28]

JOHNSTONE, PETER, a shipmaster in Bergen, Norway, in 1699. [NAS.RD3.90.669]

JOHNSTONE,......, an officer of Mackay's Regiment, in Danish service 1626, in Swedish service 1629. [TGSI.VIII.188]

JORGENSON, ADAM, from Orkney, a burgess of Bergen, Norway, in 1619. [POAS.XIII.39]

KEILLER, ALEXANDER, born 1804 in Dundee son of James Keiller, settled in Gothenburg, Sweden, as a merchant and industrialist, founder of the Gotaverken shipyard, died there in 1874. [NS#7/1/24][SE#120][SIS#70]

KEITH, ANDREW, son of Robert Keith, entered Swedish service in 1568, in 1574 appointed as Commandant of Vadstena Castle, married Elisabeth Birgersdotter Grip around 1573, settled in Stockholm, dead by 1600. [SIS#20]

KEITH, WILLIAM, Major of Mackay's Regiment, in Danish service 1626, in Swedish service 1629. [TGSI.VIII.186]

KEITH, ..., a Lieutenant of Mackay's Regiment, in Danish service 1626, in Swedish service 1629, killed at New Brandenburg in 1631 [TGSI.VIII.187]

KENNEDY, ANTHONY, a burgher of Gothenburg, Sweden, around 1630. [SE#112]

KENNEDY, Dr CHARLES, a physician in 'Santa Cruz', (Saint Croix, Danish West Indies,?), married Margaret Cooper, daughter of Arthur Cooper in 'Santa Cruz', in Eyemouth, Berwickshire, during October 1797. [EEC#392]

KENNEDY, Captain JOHN, husband of Mary ...., probate 26 May 1779 Christiansted, Danish West Indies. [RAK:CCC.XVII.132]

KENNY, ANDREW, in St Croix, Danish West Indies, graduated MD from Edinburgh University in 1812. [EMG#45]

KENNY, JOHN, probate 23 December 1772 Christiansted, Danish West Indies. [RAK: CXL.VIII.45]

KERR, DAVID JOHNSON, a cooper from Scotland, admitted as a burgess of Bergen, Norway, in 1627. [SAB]

KERR, WILLIAM, Captain of Mackay's Regiment, in Danish service 1626, in Swedish service 1629, wounded at Eckernfiord. [TGSI.VIII.186]

KERR, Dr WILLIAM, in St Croix, Danish West Indies, died in St Kitts on 8 December 1837. [AJ#4700]

KEY, THOMAS, was buried in St Peter's, Malmo, Sweden, on 18 November 1601. [SAM]

KIDD, THOMAS, son of Andrew Kidd, a tailor in Dundee, and his wife Helen Brydie, a traveller in Ystad, Denmark, 1612. [Dundee Archives, CBIII.124]

KINCH, THOMAS, from Kirkwall, Orkney, a burgess of Bergen, Norway, in 1639. [SAB]

KING, Sir JAMES, of Duck, born 1589 son of David King, to Sweden in 1609, a General under Gustavus Adolphus, returned to Scotland in 1639, fought for Charles I at the Battle of Marston Moor, died in Stockholm on 9 June 1652. [AUR.34.119][SHR.IX.40][SS#39]

KINLOCH, ..., a merchant in Gothenburg, Sweden, around 1775. [NS.11.1]

KINNAIRD, JAMES or JAKOB, a master mariner, and his wife Elizabeth Wedderburne, arrived in Gothenburg, Sweden, via Denmark in the 1630s. [SE#112]

KINNEAR, WILLIAM, a merchant from Edinburgh, applied to become a burgess of Bergen, Norway, in 1708. [SAB]

KIRKNESS, ALEXANDER, a merchant in Bergen, Norway, and a udaller in Kirkness, Orkney, 1630. [NAS.RS43.IV.119]

KNOX, HUGH, author and Presbyterian minister in 'Santa Cruz', (Saint Croix, Danish West Indies,?), was admitted as a Doctor of Divinity at Marischal College, Aberdeen, on 25 November 1773. [MCA.II.353]

KNOX, PETER JOHN, son of Henry Knox in St Croix, Danish West Indies, was educated at King's College, Aberdeen, 1777-1781. [KCA#2/353]

LADEMACHER,(?), WALTER, from Fraserburgh, Aberdeenshire, a burgess of Bergen, Norway, in 1655. [SAB]

LAING, D., a soldier of the 1st Company of Cockburn's Regiment in Swedish service, 1609. [SIS#217]

LAING, JOHN, a planter in St Croix, Danish West Indies, died on 24 August 1851, testament confirmed in 1852. [NAS.SC70.1.74]

LAKERSON, DAVID, from Orkney, a burgess of Bergen, Norway, in 1617. [SAB][POAS.XIII.39]

LAMINGTON, ANDREW, (Anders Lamiton), a merchant in Stockholm, Sweden, during the 1580s. [SIS#24]

LANG, JESSIE MORRIS, youngest daughter of Robert Lang in Largs, Ayrshire, died in St Croix, Danish West Indies, on 14 September 1842. [SG.XI.1080][GSP#779]

LANG, JOHN, in St Croix, Danish West Indies, was granted the lands of Knockewart on 17 March 1851. [NAS.RGS.247.4.8]

LANG, ROBERT, in St Croix, Danish West Indies, 1790. [Caribbeana#5/265]

LANG, WILLIAM, in St Croix, Danish West Indies, 1790. [Caribbeana#5/265]

LAUDER, WILLIAM, from Shetland, a burgess of Bergen, Norway, in 1620. [POAS.XIII.39]

LAWSON, WILLIAM, a burgess of Copenhagen, Denmark, in 1593. [MSC.II.26]

LEARMONTH, JOHN, brother of Lord Balcomie, Captain of Mackay's Regiment in Danish service 1626, killed at Boitzenberg in July 1627. [TGSI.VIII.186]

LEARMONTH, JOHN, in Danish military service at Gelnckstadt, 1 August 1628. [NAS.RH15.43.36]

LEARMONTH, WILLIAM, from Edinburgh, a burgess of Bergen, Norway, in 1672. [SAB]

LEE, ANDREW ROBERTSON, (Anders Roberdtzen Laae), from Dysart, Fife, burgess of Bergen, Norway, in 1619. [SAB]

LEIGHTON, ROBERT, a Colonel in Swedish Service, applied to the Privy Council for, and was given, a birth brief on 17 February 1686. [RPCS.IV.527]

LESLIE, Sir ALEXANDER, later Earl of Leven, born 1582 son of George Leslie, a Captain in the Dutch-Spanish war 1605, a Swedish Army officer from 1608-1638, fought in Russia, Colonel of a Swedish Regiment from 1623 to 1629, Major General and Commandant of Stralsund in 1632, Major General in the service of Sweden in Lower Saxony by 1635, returned to Scotland in 1638, led the Scots Covenanter army in its invasion of England in 1639, died in Balgonie, Fife, during 1661. [NAS.GD26.3.215/221][SHR.IX.40][SIS#41]

LESLIE, DAVID, a Swedish Army officer under Gustavus Adolphus. [SHR.ix.40]

LESLIE, JAMES or JACOB, a burgher of Ny Lodose, Sweden, by the 1590s. [SIS#24]

LESLIE, WILLIAM, probate 9 February 1772 Christiansted, Danish West Indies. [RAK:CL.XII.111]

LEWIS, THOMAS, an ironmaster from Scotland who established the Bergsund Mechanical Works at Sodermalm near Stockholm, Sweden, in 1769. [SHR.XXV.296]

LEYS, JOHN, born in Aberdeen during 1791, an engineer who emigrated to Toronto, Canada, in 1826, died in St Croix, Danish West Indies, on 8 April 1846. [AJ#5133]

LICHTOUN, JOHN, a burgess of Aberdeen in 1644, Lieutenant Colonel under General Stolhouse in Sweden. [ABR]

LINDSAY, HENRY, an officer of Mackay's Regiment, in Danish service 1626, in Swedish service 1629, later a Lieutenant Colonel in Leslie's Regiment. [TGSI.VIII.188]

LINDSAY, JAMES, (Jakob Linsaj), a merchant in Gothenburg, Sweden, 1619, a burgher of Gothenburg around 1630, sometime in Marstrand, Sweden. [SE#54/112]

LINDSAY, JOHN, of Bainshaw, born 1603, grandson of David Lindsay, 1oth Earl of Crawford, a Lieutenant Colonel of Lord Reay's Highlanders in Swedish service, killed at the Siege of New Brandenburg during 1631. [SHR.ix.50][TGSI.VIII.185]

LINDSAY, JOHN or HANS, a burgher of Gothenburg, Sweden, around 1630. [SE#112]

LINDSAY, JOHN, probate 11 November 1772 Christiansted, Danish West Indies. [RAK: C.XXII.390]

LINDSAY, RICHARD, probate 11 April 1781 Christiansted, Danish West Indies. [RAK: CCCL.XVI.123]

LINKLETTER, THOMAS, husband of Maria Willcocks, probate 1750 St Croix, Danish West Indies. [RAK]

LITTLE, ALEXANDER, probate 10 June 1748 St Croix, Danish West Indies. [RAK: 1747-1754, fo.150]

LIVINGSTON, JOHN, (Johan Levingston), an officer of the Danish Force in Ireland, 1689-1691. [DFI#146]

LIVINGSTONE, WILLIAM, probate 31 August 1770 Fredericksted, Danish West Indies. [RAK: fo.50]

LOCKHART, HUGH, (Haagen Laakertt), from Scotland, a burgess of Bergen, Norway, in 1614. [SAB]

LOGAN, WILLIAM WILLIAMSON, from Aberdeen, admitted as a burgess of Bergen, Norway, in 1625. [SAB]

LOGIE, GEORGE, Swedish Consul General in Algiers, and his son Robert, 1751. [NAS.RD3.211.2.410]

LOUTTIT, THOMAS, a udaller in Button, parish of Ireland, Orkney, then a brabiner in Bergen, Norway, 1634. [NAS.RS43.5.189]

LUMSDEN, J., an assistant Ensign of the 1st Company of Cockburn's Regiment in Swedish service, 1609. [SIS#217]

LUMSDEN, ROBERT, an officer of Mackay's Regiment, in Danish service 1626, in Swedish service 1629. [TGSI.VIII.188]

LUMSDEN, WILLIAM, Captain of Mackay's Regiment, in Danish service 1626, "sole survivor of the Massacre of Bredenburg". [TGSI.VIII.186]

LYELL, DAVID, son of Patrick Lyell a baillie of Arbroath, Angus, settled in Stockholm, Sweden, in 1638 as a merchant. [SHR.xxv.295]

LYELL, JAMES, son of Patrick Lyell a baillie of Arbroath, Angus, settled in Stockholm, Sweden, in 1638 as a merchant. [SHR.xxv.295]

LYELL, HENRY, son of Patrick Lyell a baillie of Arbroath, Angus, settled in Stockholm, Sweden, in 1638 as a merchant. [SHR.xxv.295]

LYELL, JOHN, born 1836, died in 'Santa Cruz', Danish West Indies, on 18 March 1856. [Dundee, Howff g/s]

MCARA, JEAN, eldest daughter of James McAra a merchant in Largs, Ayrshire, married Thomas Walker a surgeon from Kinross, in St Thomas, Danish West Indies, during 1813. [EA#5134/13]

MCARTHUR, JOHN, born in Argyll, died in St Croix, Danish West Indies, during 1808. [EA#4700]

MACBEAN, AENEAS, on St Thomas, Danish West Indies, husband of Johanna Mackintosh, Inverness, 13 November 1798. [NAS.RS37.619]

MACBEAN, AENEAS, jr., of Tomatin, a merchant from Glasgow, died in St Thomas, Danish West Indies, on 28 June 1810. [EA#4873/167][IJ:7.9.1810]

MACBEAN, CAROLINE, only child of Aeneas MacBean of Tomatin and St Thomas, married Lieutenant Colonel Robert Ross of the 4th Irish Dragoon Guards, in Inverness on 7 April 1819. [GM#88/368][EA#5778/233]

MACBEAN, DONALD, a farm manager who died on 24 August 1830, probate St Jan, Danish West Indies. [RAK: 1826-1836, fos.63-71]

MACBEAN, WILLIAM, in St Croix, Danish West Indies, 1790. [Caribbeana#5/265]

MCCANN, ARTHUR, probate March 1772 Christiansted, Danish West Indies. [RAK]

MCCAUL, JOHN, second son of John McCaul a merchant in Glasgow, educated at Glasgow University in 1799, at Oxford University in 1810, a merchant in St Croix, Danish West Indies, HM Consul in St Croix, 1819, died in Cane Valley, St Croix, on 16 March 1860. [Caribbeana#4.79] [NAS.GD51.6.2030] [NAS.CS17.1.40/571]

MCCLELLANE, SAMUEL, a shipmaster from Edinburgh, applied to become a burgess of Bergen, Norway, in 1705, [SAB]; a merchant in Bergen, 1707. [NAS.GD106.325]

MCCORMICK, JOHN, born in Scotland during 1794, a Presbyterian, a planter on Petersminde Estate, St Croix, Danish West Indies, by 1841. [1841 Census]

MCDERMOT, ANDREW, probate 18 December 1771 Christiansted, Danish West Indies. [RAK: L.XII.154]

MCDONALD, TERENCE, a Roman Catholic priest who died on 10 November 1775, probate St Jan, Danish West Indies. [RAK: 1758-1775, fos. 222-225]

MCDONNAL, Dr WILLIAM, probate 31 December 1771 Christiansted, Danish West Indies. [RAK: fo.162]

MCDOUGALL, GEORGE GORDON, born 1798, St Croix, Danish West Indies, drowned at Largs, Ayrshire, on 20 October 1835. [Largs g/s]

MCDOUGALL, Mrs NELLY, wife of William McDougall, probate 31 August 1768, Fredericksted, Danish West Indies. [RAK:fo.48]

MCDOUGALL, WILLIAM, probate 21 August 1782 Christiansted, Danish West Indies. [RAK: CCCC.XXVI.365]

MCDOWELL, Colonel ALEXANDER, in Sweden, was admitted as a burgess and guildsbrother of Glasgow on 6 September 1720. [Glasgow Burgess Roll]

MCDOWELL, Dr WILLIAM, probate 8 July 1755 St Croix, Danish West Indies. [RAK]

MCEVOY, CHRISTOPHER, born 1760, a planter in the Danish West Indies who later settled in Copenhagen, Denmark, died 1838. [SS#491]

MCEVOY, MICHAEL, in St Croix, Danish West Indies, 1790. [Caribbeana#5/265]

MCFARLANE, DANIEL, probate 25 January 1766 Fredericksted, Danish West Indies. [RAK: 1826-1836, fos.30-43]

MCFARLANE, DANIEL, a merchant in St Croix, Danish West Indies, co-owner of the Peggy of Greenock, 236 tons, in 1784. [Greenock Ship Register]; in St Croix, 1790. [Caribbeana#5/265]

MCFARLANE, DAVID, in St Croix, Danish West Indies, 1790. [Caribbeana#5/265]

MCFARLANE, DAVID, born around 1737, 'fifty years in the West Indies', died in Cotton Valley, St Croix, Danish West Indies, on 8 January 1808. [SM#70/317][NLS.8793/31]

MCFARLANE, GEORGE, from St Croix, Danish West Indies, graduated MD from Edinburgh University on 13 September 1803. [AJ#2906][EMG#35]

MCFARLANE, MARGARET, wife of David McFarlane, died in Cotton Valley, St Croix, Danish West Indies, on 4 September 1803. [EEC#14337]

MCFARLANE, WALTER, a merchant in St Croix, Danish West Indies, 1776-1778. [NLS.8793/4]

MACFIE, JANET, in Karsam, Sweden, 5 July 1832. [NAS.RD.Renfrew, #13/78]

MCGEE, REBECCA, died on 18 December 1827, probate St Jan, Danish West Indies. [RAK: 1826-1836, fos.30-43]

MCGILLIVRAY, DONALD, probate 28 February 1781 Christiansted, Danish West Indies. [RAK:CCXC.VII.82]

MCILROY, ARCHIBALD, probate 27 April 1768 Christiansted, Danish West Indies. [RAK: XIV.29]

MACINTOSH, ALEXANDER, probate 11 April 1767 Fredericksted, Danish West Indies. [RAK]

MACINTOSH, JOHN, probate 30 April 1768 Christiansted, Danish West Indies. [RAK:XXXXX]

MACKAY, ALEXANDER, son of John Mackay and Margaret Munro, a Major of the Swedish Army in Pomerania, died at Strathan-Tongue, Scotland, in 1770. [Book of Mackay#325]

MACKAY, DANIEL, in 'Santa Cruz', (Saint Croix, Danish West Indies), married Mrs Muir, widow of John Muir late in Demerara, in Morningside, Edinburgh, on 5 August 1808. [SM#71/78][GM#95/273]; born 1757, late in St Croix, Danish

West Indies, died in Glebeside Row, Glasgow, on 15 May 1839. [SG.8.768]

MACKAY, DONALD, Lord Reay, Colonel of Mackay's Regiment, in Danish service 1626, in Swedish service, 1629. [TGSI.VIII.228] [NAS.GD84.2.174/175/177/180/181/183/185/186]

MACKAY, HUGH, an officer of Mackay's Regiment, in Danish service 1626, in Swedish service 1629. [TGSI.VIII.188]

MACKAY, IYE, son of William Mackay of Bighouse, Captain of Mackay's Regiment, in Danish service 1626, in Swedish service 1629. [TGSI.VIII.187]

MACKAY, Sir PATRICK, of Lairg, Captain of Mackay's Regiment, in Danish service 1626, died of wounds received at Oldenburg in October 1627. [TGSI.VIII.186]

MACKAY, ROBERT, a soldier of the 1st Company of Cockburn's Regiment, in Danish service 1626, died of wounds received at Oldenburg during October 1627. [TGSI.VIII.186]

MACKAY, WILLIAM, son of Donald Mackay of Scourie, Captain of Mackay's Regiment, in Danish service 1626, in Swedish service 1629, later a Lieutenant Colonel of the Swedish Army, killed at the Battle of Lutzen on 6 November 1632. [TGSI.VIII.187]

MACKAY, WILLIAM, Captain of Mackay's Regiment, in Danish service 1626, in Swedish service 1629. [TGSI.VIII.187]

MACKAY, ..., Lieutenant of Mackay's Regiment, in Danish service 1626, in Swedish service 1629, later promoted in Ruthven's Regiment. [TGSI.VIII.187]

MCKECHNIE, ALEXANDER, of Little Batturich, Dunbartonshire, a merchant in Glasgow, later in St Croix, Danish West Indies, 6 January 1769. [NAS.RS10.187]

MCKENZIE, ALEXANDER, died on 24 April 1762, probate 1767 Christiansted, Danish West Indies, also Fredericksted, Danish West Indies. [RAK: 1760-1775, FOS.9-10]

MCKENZIE, COLIN, probate 8 January 1777 Christiansted, Danish West Indies. [RAK: CCC.V.102]

MCKENZIE, MURDOCH, educated at Marischal College, Aberdeen, graduated MA in 1622, chaplain to Mackay's Regiment, in Danish service 1626, in Swedish service 1629, fought under Gustavus Adolphus prior to 1645, later minister of Suddie, Ross-shire. [TGSI.VIII.189][F.7.17]

MCKENZIE, THOMAS, brother of the Earl of Seaforth, Captain of Mackay's Regiment, in Danish service 1626, in Swedish service 1629, wounded at Eckenfiord. [TGSI.VIII.87]

MCKEY, PETER, probate 24 March 1773 Christiansted, Danish West Indies. [RAK: CL.XXX.178]

MACKIE, CHARLES, commander of a Swedish sloop in 1759. [PRO.SP54.45.100B]

MCLARAN, JOHN, probate 1777 Christiansted, Danish West Indies. [RAK: CCCL.XVIII.264]

MCLARTY, MALCOLM, born 1845, son of Malcolm McLarty and his wife Helen Gow Thomson, died in St Croix, Danish West Indies, on 10 February 1863. [Port Glasgow g/s]

MCLAUGHLAN, CHARLES, probate 8 April 1772 Christiansted, Danish West Indies. [RAK: XC.VII.307]

MCLAUGHLAND, ALLAN, probate 7 May 1777 Christiansted, Danish West Indies. [RAK: CCXC.I.52]

MCLEAN, JOHN, son of McLean of Duart, banker and merchant in Gothenburg, Sweden, from around 1619, enobled under the name Macaleer in 1649, died in Gothenburg during 1666. [SHR.xxv.290]

MCLEAN, JOHN, died on 24 April 1762, probate 1767 Christiansted, also in Fredericksted, Danish West Indies. [RAK: 1760-1775,fo.10]

MACLEISH, ROBERT, a shipmaster from Dunbar, applied to be a burgess of Bergen, Norway, in 1737. [SAB]

MCLENNAN, MICHAEL, probate 20 June 1761 Christiansted, Danish West Indies. [RAK.fo.318]

MCLEOD, NORMAN, a merchant who died in St Thomas, Danish West Indies, on 23 May 1805. [SM#67/805][AJ#3015]

MCLINTOCK, LAWRENCE, probate 16 December 1772 Christiansted, Danish West Indies. [RAK:CL.X.107]

MCMICHAEL, ROBERT, probate 31 October 1768 Fredericksted, Danish West Indies. [RAK]

MCNEIL, NEIL, a merchant in St Kitts, later in St Croix, around 1780. [NAS.CS237.T4/1]

MCNEIL, ..., probate 20 July 1765 Fredericksted, Danish West Indies. [RAK]

MCPHERSON, DANIEL, probate 10 June 1748 St Croix, Danish West Indies. [RAK: 1747-1754, fo.135]

MACRORRY, J., a soldier of the 1st Company of Cockburn's Regiment in Swedish service 1609. [SIS#217]

MACRUDDERY, W., a soldier of the 2nd Company of Cockburn's Regiment in Swedish service, 1609. [SIS#217]

MAGNUS, GUSTAVE, Baron d'Armfelt, born 1792 in Stockholm, Sweden, arrived via Stockton, residing in Edinburgh by June 1807. [ECA.SL115.2.2/58]

MAIN, JOHN THOMASON, a cooper from Orkney, a burgess of Bergen, Norway, in 1630. [SAB]

MAITLAND, JAMES, in Careston, Angus, a Jacobite chaplain in 1745, escaped to Gothenburg, Sweden, in 1746. [GK#115][SHR.lxx.64]

MANSON, ALEXANDER, a weaver from Orkney, a burgess of Bergen, Norway, in 1626. [SAB]

MANSON, ANDREW, from Orkney, a burgess of Bergen, Norway, in 1614. [SAB]

MANSON, DAVID, from Orkney, a burgess of Bergen, Norway, in 1630. [SAB]

MANSON, EDWARD, from Kirkwall, Orkney, a burgess of Bergen, Norway, in 1634. [SAB]

MANSON, HENRY, from Orkney, a burgess of Bergen, Norway, in 1618. [SAB][POAS.XIII.39]

MANSON, JOHN, a baker from Orkney, a burgess of Bergen, Norway, in 1641. [SAB]

MANSON, MAGNUS, from Orkney, a burgess of Bergen, Norway, in 1640. [SAB]

MANSON, MICHAEL, from Orkney, a burgess of Bergen, Norway, in 1628. [SAB]

MANSON, ..., from Orkney, a burgess of Bergen, Norway, in 1614. [POAS.XIII.39]

MARCUSON, JAMES, from Orkney, a burgess of Bergen, Norway, in 1671. [SAB]

MARSHALL, Captain THOMAS, probate 20 December 1780 Christiansted, Danish West Indies. [RAK: CCCCL.IX.94]

MARTIN, DAVID, a Lieutenant of Mackay's Regiment, in Danish service 1626, killed at Boitzenburg during July 1627. [TGSI.VIII.187]

MATSON, CHRISTIAN, from Shetland, a burgess of Bergen, Norway, in 1586. [POAS.XIII.39]

MAULE, JAMES, born 6 August 1705 in Edinburgh, possibly son of John Maule of Glithnoe, Kincardineshire, emigrated to Sweden in 1731, admitted as a burgess of Montrose, Angus, in 1742, chief mate of the Rex Sverige, the first Swedish East Indiaman, 1746. [SG.8.26][NAS.GD45.14.447]

[SE#117][Montrose Burgess Roll][SAS#114]

MAXWELL, EDWARD, probate 2 November 1774 Christiansted, Danish West Indies. [RAK: CC.XXXIII.228]

MAXWELL, J., a soldier of the 3rd Company of Cockburn's Regiment in Swedish service, 1609. [SIS#216]

MELDRUM, A., a soldier of the 1st Company of Cockburn's Regiment in Swedish service, 1609. [SIS#217]

MELDRUM, R., a soldier of the 2nd Company of Cockburn's Regiment in Swedish service, 1609. [SIS#217]

MELDRUM, THOMAS, Colonel in the service of the King of Denmark and Norway, was admitted as a burgess of Aberdeen on 29 August 1681. [APB]

MELVIN, FRANCIS, probate 31 October 1767 Fredericksted, Danish West Indies. [RAK, fo.12]

MENZIES, WILLIAM, a Jacobite cavalryman in 1746, settled in Gothenburg, Sweden, by 1747. [SHR.lxx.64]

MERCER, JAMES, (Jakob Merser), a merchant in Gothenburg, Sweden, around 1630. [SE#112]

MERCER, THOMAS, son of Robert Mercer of Aldie, Kinross, a Jacobite in 1745, cornet of Lord Nairne's Regiment, settled in Gothenburg, Sweden, by 1747. [SHR.lxx.65]

MIDDLETON, GEORGE, a resident of Christianshavn, Copenhagen, Zealand, Denmark, 1658. [Aberdeen Shore Works Accounts, p.418]

MIDDLETON, JOHN, (Hans Middeltun), a farmworker, was buried in St Peter's, Malmo, Sweden,1546. [SAM]

MIDDLETON, NATHANIEL, shipmaster of the Pelican of Bergen in 1694. [NAS.RS43.83.103]

MIDDLETON, WILLIAM, probate 26 November 1769 Christiansted, Danish West Indies. [RAK: fo.162]

MILL, ROBERT, from Montrose, Angus, a burgess of Bergen, Norway, in 1695. [SAB]

MILL, ROBERT, (Rubbert Maell), from Musselburgh near Edinburgh, a burgess of Bergen, Norway, in 1655. [SAB]

MILL, THOMAS, from Aberdeen, a burgess of Bergen, Norway, 1632. [SAB]

MILL, WILLIAM, (Willumb Meell), from Aberdeen, a burgess of Bergen, Norway, in 1631. [SAB]

MILLER, J., a soldier of the 2nd Company of Cockburn's Regiment in Swedish service, 1609. [SIS#217]

MILNE, ALEXANDER, son of Peter Milne in Old Meldrum, Aberdeenshire, died in St Croix, Danish West Indies, during 1810.[EA#4900]

MITCHELL, DAVID, from Montrose, a merchant in Gothenburg, Sweden, who died in 1803. [SE#119]

MITCHELL, HUGH, sr., a planter, died on 3 February 1758, husband of Maria Matthews, probate St Jan, Danish West Indies. [RAK:1758-1775, fo.1a]

MITCHELL, JOHN, probate 1 February 1767 Christiansted, Danish West Indies. [RAK]

MITCHELL, ROBERT, probate 30 January 1782 Christiansted, Danish West Indies. [RAK: CCC.XXXI.174]

MITCHELL, WILLIAM, died on 12 February 1802, probate St Jan, Danish West Indies. [RAK: 1797-1807, fos.23-33]

MITCHELL, WILLIAM, born 1763 in East Seaton, St Vigeans, Arbroath, settled in St Croix during 1784, a merchant in St Croix, Danish West Indies, died at Buss End, St Croix, on 16 March 1834. [NAS.S/H][AJ#4514]

MITCHELLSON, JOHN, (Hans Mitchellssen), from Aberdeen, admitted as a burgess of Bergen, Norway, in 1619. [SAB]

MITCHELLSON, JOHN, from Fraserburgh, (Fridtzel?), Aberdeenshire, was admitted as a burgess of Bergen, Norway, in 1626. [SAB]

MITCHELLSON, JOHN, from Scotland, admitted as a burgess of Bergen, Norway, in 1628. [SAB]

MOFFAT, ROBERT, a Captain of the Swedish Army, who settled in Sweden and was granted a birth brief in 1672. [RPCS.II.573]

MOGENSDOTTER, ANNE, deceased by 1601, a burgess of Bergen, Norway, and owner of Findeland, Hillisuig, Shetland. [PSAS.XIV.32/33]

MOIR, Dr ALEXANDER, born in Mortlich, Banffshire, a physician in St Croix, Danish West Indies, graduated MD from King's College, Aberdeen, on 27 September 1763, died in St Croix during November 1766. [KCA#131][FAB#207][SM#28/615][AJ#987]

MOIR, CHARLES, a Jacobite in 1745, Captain of Lord Lewis Gordon's Regiment, settled in Gothenburg, Sweden, by 1747. [SHR.lxx.64]

MOIR, JAMES, of Stoneywood, born 1719 son of James Moir and his wife Jedan Erskine, married Margaret Mackenzie at Ardross in 1740, a supercargo of the Swedish East India Company, Jacobite Governor of Aberdeen in 1745, settled in Gothenburg in 1746, a merchant there, enobled in Sweden, pardoned in 1762, returned to Scotland, died 29 September 1784. [SHR.lxx.64][Goteborgs Landsarkiver, 1755]

MONCREIFF, WILLIAM, (Willem Munkrij or Magkryff), Captain of cavalry at Wesenberg 1573, settled in Marstrand, Sweden, by 1588. [SIS#23]

MONCRIEFF, ..., Captain of Mackay's Regiment, in Danish service 1626, in Swedish service 1629, killed at New Brandenburg. [TGSI.VIII.187]

MONCUR, HANS or JOHN, served in William Colquhoun's troop of horse in Sweden around 1569, later, by 1587, he was a country merchant in Vastmanland, Sweden. [SIS#23]

MONORGAN, J., a soldier of the 2nd Company of Cockburn's Regiment in Swedish service, 1609. [SIS#217]

MONTGOMERIE, MOULD & FENWICK, merchants in Stockholm, Sweden,1726. [JSL#250]

MONTGOMERIE, ROBERT, a merchant in St Croix, Danish West Indies, in 1809, later in Irvine, Ayrshire. [NAS.CS239/S.49/9]

MONTGOMERIE, ROBERT, in St Thomas, Danish West Indies, testament confirmed in Edinburgh 1824. [NAS.SC70.1.31]

MONTGOMERIE, WILLIAM EWING, son of John Montgomerie and his wife Marion Paterson in Ardrossan, Ayrshire, settled in St Croix, Danish West Indies, married .... McPherson, and died on 13 August 1835. [HCA.1.231]

MONTGOMERY, ADAM, in Stockholm, dead by 7 November 1732, brother of John Montgomery yr., a merchant in Campbeltown, [Argyll Sheriff Court Book #X]

MONTGOMERY, DUNCAN, in St Croix, Danish West Indies, 1790. [Caribbeana#5/265]

MONTGOMERY, JOHN, born 1701, settled in Sweden, husband of Anna Campbell, a factory owner in Sweden and Finland, died about 1760. [SHR,xxv.294]

MORRIS, JOHN, a merchant in St Croix, Danish West Indies, from 1776 to 1784, later in Irvine, Ayrshire. [NAS.NRAS#0396.TD248]

MORRISON, JOHN, a soldier of Cockburn's Regiment in Swedish service, 1609. [SIS#216]

MORRISON, JOHN, (Joen Mouritzon), from Stirling, a burgess of Bergen, Norway, in 1619. [SAB]

MORTIMER, GILBERT, son of Andrew Mortimer a burgess of Dundee and his wife Christian Small, settled in Stubbekobing, Denmark, by 1607. [Dundee birthbrief, CBIII/69]

MORTIMER, JANET, daughter of Andrew Mortimer a burgess of Dundee and his wife Christian Small, settled in Stubbekobing, Denmark, by 1607. [Dundee birthbrief, CBIII/69]

MORTON, WALTER, son of Hugh Martin in Leith, died in St Croix, Danish West Indies, on 5 July 1797. [EEC#416]

MOWAT, ANDREW, in Shetland, granted a licence to marry in Bergen, Norway, on 17 June 1587. [NLS.Adv.MS#35.5.1]

MOWAT, ANDREW, of Howgland, a Scot residing in 'Gereisweycke', Norway, 1591, 1598. [CSP.Scot.x.553] [NAS.RD1.101.352]

MOWAT, HUGH, an officer of Mackay's Regiment, in Danish service 1626, in Swedish service 1629. [TGSI.VIII.188]

MOWATT, HAROLD JOHN, a Lieutenant of the 64th Regiment, died in St Croix, Danish West Indies, during 1801. [AJ#2807]

MUDIE, GEORGE JAMES, born 1802, son of John Young Mudie a burgess of Edinburgh 1815, settled in St Croix in 1821. [MD]

MUDIE, JOHN, born 1813, son of John Young Mudie a burgess of Edinburgh, settled in St Croix. [MD]

MUDIE, JOHN JAMIESON, (Joen Jacobssen Myddy), a weaver from Kirkwall, Orkney, a burgess of Bergen, Norway, in 1654. [SAB]

MUIR, ANDREW, in St Croix, Danish West Indies, later in Glasgow, testament confirmed with the Commissariat of Glasgow on 14 December 1814. [NAS.CC9.78.633]

MUIR, CHRISTIAN, in Bergen, Norway, 1632. [NAS.RS43.4.234]

MUIR, ROBERT, Captain of the 3rd Company of Cockburn's
Regiment in Swedish service, 1609. [SIS#217]

MULDROP, CHRISTIAN, late Consul for the King of Denmark at
Leith, testament confirmed on 25 January 1769 and on 1
September 1769 with the Commissariat of Edinburgh. [NAS]

MUNRO, ANDREW, Captain of Mackay's Regiment in Danish
service 1626, killed in a duel at Femern. [TGSI.VIII.187]

MUNRO, ANDREW, an officer of Mackay's Regiment, in Danish
service 1626, in Swedish service 1629, killed at Oldenburg.
[TGSI.VIII.187]

MUNRO, DAVID, Major of Mackay's Regiment, in Danish service
1626, in Swedish service 1629, "scorched by powder at
Eckenfiord". [TGSI.VIII.186]

MUNRO, DAVID, an officer of Mackay's Regiment, in Danish
service 1626, in Swedish service 1629, wounded at
Oldenburg. [TGSI.VIII.188]

MUNRO, FARQUHAR, an officer of Mackay's Regiment, in
Danish service 1626, in Swedish service 1629, killed at
Oldenburg.[TGSI.VIII.188]

MUNRO, HECTOR, of Foulis, Captain of Mackay's Regiment, in
Danish service 1626, in Swedish service 1629, Colonel of
the Swedish Army by the 1630s.
[TGSI.VIII.187][RGS#IX.112]

MUNRO, HECTOR, an officer of the Danish Force in Ireland,
1689-1691. [DFI#146]

MUNRO, JOHN, a soldier of the 1st Company of Cockburn's
Regiment in Swedish service, 1609. [SIS#217]

MUNRO, JOHN, of Obisdell, Captain of Mackay's Regiment, in
Danish service 1626, in Swedish service 1629, later Colonel
of a Scots Regiment. [TGSI.VIII.187]

MUNRO, JOHN, Assynt, Captain of Mackay's Regiment, in
Danish service 1626, in Swedish service 1629.
[TGSI.VIII.187]

MUNRO, ROBERT, of Foulis, Captain of Mackay's Regiment, in
Danish service 1626, in Swedish service 1629, later a
Colonel of the Swedish Army.
[RGS.IX.112][TGSI.VIII.187][SS#79]

MUNRO, ROBERT, of Contullich, a Colonel in Danish service,
later fought for Sweden in Germany around 1634.
[RGS.IX.111][TGSI.VIII.185]

MURRAY, ALEXANDER, a soldier of the 1st Company of
Cockburn's Regiment in Swedish service, 1609. [SIS#217]

MURRAY, ALEXANDER, a burgher of Gothenburg, Sweden,
around 1630. [SE#112]

MURRAY, HUGH, an officer of Mackay's Regiment, in Danish
service 1626, in Swedish service 1629. [TGSI.VIII.189]

MURRAY, JAMES, probate 31 August 1767 Fredericksted,
Danish West Indies. [RAK: fo.12]

MURRAY, JOHN, son of Alexander Murray, a burgess of Turriff,
Aberdeenshire, husband of Margaret Lindsay, was admitted
as a burgess of Kalmar, Sweden, in 1597. [MSC.II.41]

MURRAY, ROBERT, in Bergen, Norway, 1630. [NAS.RS43.4.171]

NAIRN, WILLIAM, Captain of the Swedish India ship Calmar, died
on 25 March 1743 off St Helena on the voyage home.
[SM.V.295]

NAIRNE, HENRY, son of John Nairne, third Lord Nairne, a
Lieutenant of the French Royal Ecossais, a Jacobite in
1746, settled in Gothenburg, Sweden, by 1747. [SHR.lxx.65]

NAIRNE, JOHN, third Lord Nairne, eldest son of Lord William
Murray and Margaret Nairne, Jacobite in 1715 and in 1745,
escaped to Gothenburg, Sweden, in 1746, later settled in

France, died there in 1770, husband of Lady Catherine Murray. [SHR.lxx.65]

NANNING, HENRICK, harpooner on the whaling ship <u>Prince of Wales of Leith</u> to Greenland in 1753. [NAS.E508.50.8]

NAPIER, JAMES, died on 28 July 1758, husband of (1) Rebecca ...., (2) Mary ....., probate 1 June 1761 Christiansted, Danish West Indies. [RAK: 1755-1761]

NAPIER, MARY, wife of (1) John Napier, (20 Alexander Brabner, probate Christiansted, Danish West Indies. [RAK.1755-1761]

NEAF, JAMES, son of John Neaf of Kinereit and Methie, and his wife Janet Wishart , emigrated to Sweden, Governor of Westmanland and Dalarne, killed in 1598. [SG.7.27]

NEILSON, CHARLES, from Galloway, a burgess of Bergen, Norway, in 1719. [SAB]

NEILSON, PETER, a merchant in Christianna, Norway, in 1684. [NAS.RD2.63.5]

NICHOLSON, ARCHIBALD, a soldier of the 1st Company of Cockburn's Regiment in Swedish service 1609. [SIS#217]

NIDDRY, THOMAS, son of John Niddry and his wife Christine Christie in Kirktonhill, settled as a weaver in Koge, Denmark, died by 1625. [Angus Archives, M/WA/24]

NIELSON, GABRIEL, from Orkney, a burgess of Bergen, Norway, in 1623. [SAB][POAS.XIII.39]

NIELSON, THOMAS, from Orkney, a burgess of Bergen, Norway, in 1613. [SAB][POAS.XII.39]

NIELSON, ..., from Orkney, a burgess of Bergen, Norway, in 1576. [POAS.XIII.39]

NISBET, WILLIAM, born 1596, to Sweden as an Army officer, died in Upsalla, Sweden, during 1660. [SHR.IX.274]

NISEN, HANS, harpooner on the whaling ship <u>Campbeltown of Leith</u> to Greenland in 1753. [NAS.E508.50.8/7]

NORES, JOHN, a merchant in Christiansund, Norway, a burgess of Montrose, Angus, 1760. [Montrose Burgess Roll]

NORMANSON, STEPHEN, in Housland, Norway, husband of Anna Olasdochter, in Shetland, 1623. [NAS.RS44.2.35]

NORRIE, GORDON, a merchant, married Maria Craig of Gothenburg, there on 4 January 1815. [SM#77.159]

NORSK, MAGNUS, minister of Yell, Shetland Islands, from 1586, then minister of Unst, Shetland Islands, from 1593, married Dorothie Thomasdaughter, parents of Thomas, Robert, Patrick, Olaf, and Magnus; he died in May 1632. [F.7.298]

NORUNE, GEORGE, in Rumsdel, Norway, 1632. [Aberdeen Sheriff Court decree book III, 1 June 1632]

OGILVIE, GEORGE, (Joran Ugleby), a merchant in Gothenburg, Sweden, around 1630. [SE#112]

OGILVIE, JAMES, in St Croix, Danish West Indies, 1765. [NAS.AC.Decreets, Vol.51, 19.7.1765]

OGILVIE, THOMAS, (Thomas Uglebie), settled in Nykoping, Sweden, by 1600. [SIS#23]

OGILVY, DAVID, a merchant in Coul, Tannadice, Angus, a Jacobite and Captain of Ogilvy's Regiment in 1745, escaped from Dundee to Bergen, Norway, in 1746, later moved to France. [OR.2/127][LPR#228]

OGILVY, JAMES, miller at the Mill of Inshewan, Tannadice, Angus, a Jacobite and Lieutenant of Ogilvy's Regiment in 1745, escaped to Bergen, Norway, in 1746, later in Sweden. [GK#117][OR5][LPR#228]

OGILVY, JOHN, son of Alexander Ogilvy and his wife Margaret Anderson in Countesswells, Aberdeenshire, settled in Copenhagen, Denmark, by 1602. [MSC.II.60]

OGILVY, JOHN, of Inshewan, Tannadice, Angus, born 1711, son of John Ogilvy and his wife Mary Keith, a Jacobite and Captain of Ogilvy's Regiment in 1745, escaped to Bergen, Norway, in 1746, settled in Gothenburg, Sweden, in 1747, later in France. [OR2][LPR228][SHR.lxx.65]

OLAFS, JACGAN, steersman on the whaling ship North Star of Dunbar to Greenland in 1752. [NAS.E508.49.8]

OLIPHANT, LAURENCE, of Gask, Perthshire, born 1691 son of James Oliphant and Janet Murray, a Jacobite in 1715 and in 1745, Lieutenant Colonel of Cavalry, Deputy Governor of Perth, escaped to Gothenburg, Sweden, in 1746, later settled in France where he died in 1767. [SHR.lxx.65]

OLIPHANT, LAURENCE, born 1724 son of Laurence Oliphant of Gask (1691-1767), a Jacobite in 1745, ADC to Prince Charles Edward Stuart, escaped to Gothenburg, Sweden, in 1747. [SHR.lxx.65]

OLLASON, JOHN, a shoemaker from Orkney, a burgess of Bergen, Norway, in 1647. [SAB]

OLLSIN, MEILIS, skipper in Malstrand, Sweden, master of the St Marie, 1668. [NAS.NRAS.0336, db2/bundle 29]

OLSEN, DAVID, from Shetland, a burgess of Bergen, Norway, in 1619. [POAS.XIII.39]

OLSEN, PETER, burgess of Elsburg, Sweden, 1555. [DCA.Burgh Court book#III]

ORCHARDTON, Sir JOHN, son of Sir Andrew Orchardton of that Ilk, Aberdeenshire, and his wife Elizabeth Robertson, Captain of the Guards of the Swedish Army, 1663. [RGS.IXI.495]

ORMSTED, JORGENLAPPELEN, born 1780 in Dram, Norway, a merchant, arrived in Gravesend on 23 September 1803, residing at the Turf Coffee House, Edinburgh, by 22 November 1803. [ECA.SL115.2.2/24]

ORNFELT, AXEL, of Gotterup, Chancellor of Denmark, 1635.
[NAS.RS44.III.258]

ORR, JAMES, probate 30 November 1774 Christiansted, Danish
West Indies. [RAK: CXC.V.24]

OSBORN, ROBERT WEIR, in St Croix, Danish West Indies, 1790.
[Caribbeana#5/265]

OSTERLUND, JOHANN, born 1767 in Helsingfors, Finland, a
Swedish captain, landed at Fraserburgh, Aberdeenshire, on
4 December 1808, residing in Leith by 1809.
[ECA.SL115.2.2/66]

OTTERBURN, J., a soldier of the 2nd Company of Cockburn's
Regiment in Swedish service, 1609. [SIS#217]

PANTER, ..., children of Samuel Panter, were buried in St
Peter's, Malmo, Sweden, in 1601. [SAM]

PANTON, WILLIAM, (Willem Pantun), was buried in St Peter's,
Malmo, Sweden, in 1600. [SAM]

PAPLAY, DAVID, from Orkney, burgess of Bergen, Norway,
1602, 1618. [NAS.RS43.I.112][POAS.XIII.39]

PARIS, JOHN, from Orkney, a burgess of Bergen, Norway, 1558.
[POAS.XIII.39]

PATERSON, JOHN, (Joen Pejthersen), a smith from Caithness, a
burgess of Bergen, Norway, in 1619. [SAB]

PATERSON, JOHN, a missionary who settled in Sweden in 1807,
founder of the Evangelical Society and the Swedish Bible
Society. [SIS#72]

PATERSON, PETER, from Dundee, a burgess of Bergen,
Norway, in 1635. [SAB]

PATERSON, WILLIAM, probably from Kirkcaldy, Fife, then by
1627 in Bergen, Norway, grandson of William Paterson a
burgess of Kirkcaldy. [NAS.SH.1627]

PATULLO, ANDREW, a factor in Stockholm, 1689.
[RPCS.XIII.555]

PATULLO, HENRY, a merchant in Dundee, Jacobite
quartermaster in 1745, settled in Gothenburg, Sweden, by
1747. [SHR.lxx.65]

PATULLO, THOMAS, a merchant in Stockholm, Sweden, in 1706.
[NAS.GD137.3468]

PEARSON, THOMAS, master of the <u>Fortune of Copenhagen,</u>
1704. [APB]

PERCY, HENRY, a merchant in Trontheim, Norway, 1695, 1697.
[NAS.RD3.80.14.319; RD4.81.609]

PETERSEN, HENRICK, harpooner on the whaling ship <u>Peggy of</u>
<u>Glasgow</u> to Greenland in 1752. [NAS.E508.50.8]

PETERSON, ERASMUS, in Stour, Norway, husband of Martha
Olasdochter in Shetland, 1623. [NAS.RS44.2.35]

PHILP, HENRY, a merchant in Norway, deceased, father of
James apprenticed to a merchant in Edinburgh during 1679.
[Edinburgh Apprentice Register]

PHILP, JAMES, a merchant in Bergen, Norway, 1690.
[ECA.Moses.74/3299]

PIETERSEN, ANDREAS, harpooner on the whaling ship <u>North</u>
<u>Star of Dunbar</u> from Dunbar to Greenland in 1752.
[NAS.E508.49.8]

PILMURE, ROBERT, from Dundee, a merchant in Stockholm,
Sweden, testament confirmed on 15 February 1709 with the
Commissariat of Edinburgh. [NAS.CC8.8.84/324]

PIRIE, ANDREW GEORGESON, from Scotland, admitted as a
burgess of Bergen, Norway, in 1615. [SAB]

PIRIE, THOMAS, born in 1803, son of George Pirie a merchant in
Aberdeen, died in Mandal, Norway, on 19 June 1839.
[AJ#4774]

POLSON, MURDOCH, an officer of Mackay's Regiment, in Danish service 1626, in Swedish service 1629, killed at Oldenburg. [TGSI.VIII.189]

POTTINGER, WILLIAM, a burgess of Bergen, Norway, husband of Mary Tulloch, 1647. [NAS.RS43.VII.19]

PRIMROSE, JOHN, a merchant burgess of Stockholm, Sweden, 1646. [NAS.GD172.2318]

PRINGLE, GEORGE, Major in the service of Gustavus Adolphus, and husband of Elizabeth, daughter of Sir Patrick Ruthven. [F.2.15]

PURVIS, JOHN, a soldier of the 1st Company of Cockburn's Regiment in Swedish service, 1609. [SIS#217]

RAMSAY, ALEXANDER, probate 28 July 1779 Christiansted, Danish West Indies. [RAK: CCL.IX.273]

RAMSAY, GEORGE, probate 16 September 1765 Fredericksted, Danish West Indies. [RAK]

RAMSAY, Sir JAMES, born 1589, Major General of the Swedish Army, died a prisoner in Dillenburgh Castle on 11 March 1638, husband of Dame Isobel Spence testament confirmed on 15 April 1656 with the Commissariat of Edinburgh. [SHR.IX.45][SS#44]

RAMSQUOY, JOHN, from Orkney, in Bergen, Norway, 1617. [NAS.RS43.1.38]

RASMUSSON, ERASMUS, (?),from Dundee, admitted as a burgess of Bergen, Norway, in 1615. [SAB]

REID, GILES, in St Croix, Danish West Indies, 1790. [Caribbeana#5/265]

REID, JAMES, (Jacob Reidh), a burgher of Ny Lodose, Sweden, by 1590s. [SIS#24]

REID, JAMES, born 3 January 1777, son of William Reid, the town clerk of Banff, and his wife Margaret Innes, settled in Gothenborg, Sweden, as a merchant, died there on 17 March 1813. [NS#7.1.147]

REMING, JAMES, from Fraserburgh, Aberdeenshire, a burgess of Bergen, Norway, in 1669. [SAB]

RIAMERS, JAMES, from Orkney, a burgess of Bergen, Norway, in 1624. [SAB]

RICHARDSON, W., a soldier in the 1st Company of Cockburn's Regiment in Swedish service, 1609. [SIS#217]

RICHARDSON, WILLIAM, a planter, died on 9 May 1747, husband of Susanna Hasel, probate St Croix, Danish West Indies. [RAK: 1741-1748, fo.307]

RICHMOND, ROBERT, a surgeon, son of Mathew Richmond a nurseryman in Edinburgh, died in St Croix, Danish West Indies, on 22 May 1805. [SM#67/885]

ROBERTSON, ANDREW, son of William Robertson a burgess of Aberdeen and his wife Bessie Chalmer, died in Copenhagen, Denmark, around 1593. [MSC.II.26]

ROBERTSON, ANDREW, from Shetland, a burgess of Bergen, Norway, in 1597. [POAS.XIII.39]

ROBERTSON, ANDREW, from Scotland, a burgess of Bergen, Norway, in 1638. [SAB]

ROBERTSON, CHARLES, died on 2 March 1756, probate 30 March 1757 Christiansted, also St Croix, Danish West Indies. [RAK: 1747-1782, fo.33]

ROBERTSON, EDWARD, from Kirkwall, Orkney, a burgess of Bergen, Norway, in 1660. [SAB]

ROBERTSON, JAMES, from Scotland, admitted as a burgess of Bergen, Norway, in 1616. [SAB]

ROBERTSON, JAMES, born 1566, from Struan, Perthshire, settled in Sweden in 1614, an apothecary in Stockholm in 1626, enobled in 1635, physician to Queen Christina from 1639, died in 1652. [SHR#xxv.290][SIS#45]

ROBERTSON, JAMES, in St Croix, Danish West Indies, 1790. [Caribbean#5/265]

ROBERTSON, JOHN, a cooper from Leith, was admitted as a burgess of Bergen, Norway, in 1616. [SAB]

ROBERTSON, JOHN, from Banff, a burgess of Bergen, Norway, in 1636. [SAB]

ROBERTSON, JOHN, (Joen Rubbertsen), from Kirkwall, Orkney, a burgess of Bergen, Norway, in 1650. [SAB]

ROBERTSON, MAGNUS, from Orkney, a burgess of Bergen, Norway, in 1617. [SAB][POAS.XIII.39]

ROBERTSON, THOMAS, from Leith, a burgess of Bergen, Norway, in 1665. [SAB]

ROBERTSON, WALTER, from Aberdeen, a burgess of Bergen, Norway, in 1634. [SAB]

ROBERTSON, WILLIAM, from Orkney, a burgess of Bergen, Norway, in 1613. [SAB][POAS.XIII.39]

ROBERTSON, WILLIAM, from Queensferry, West Lothian, a burgess of Bergen, Norway, in 1693. [SAB]

ROBINSON, JOSEPH, probate 1750 St Croix, Danish West Indies. [RAK]

ROLLO, JAMES, a Jacobite of Prince Charles Edward Stuart's Life Guard in 1745, settled in Gothenburg, Sweden, by 1747. [SHR.lxx.65]

ROLLOSS, VOLKART, harpooner on the whaling ship Dundee of Dundee to Greenland in 1753 and in 1754. [NAS.E508.51.8]

ROSENKRANZ, JACOB, of Keidistrop, Denmark, 1636, [NAS.RS44.III.460]

ROSS, ALEXANDER, a merchant in Copenhagen, Denmark, 1719. [NAS.GD158.1788][JSL#65]

ROSS, ALEXANDER, a merchant in Sweden, was admitted as a burgess and guilds-brother of Ayr, Scotland, on 26 July 1754. [ABR]

ROSS, ANDREW, a merchant in Gothenburg, was admitted as a burgess of Perth on 21 July 1743. [NAS.GD1/772/5]

ROSS, DAVID, son of Alexander Ross of Invercarron, an officer of Mackay's Regiment, in Danish service 1626, in Swedish service 1629. [TGSI.VIII.189]

ROSS, GEORGE, in Bergen, Norway, 1751. [NAS.NRAS.2233/2]

ROSS, GEORGE, a merchant in Gothenburg, Sweden, around 1745. [Goteborgs Landsarkivet]

ROSS, HUGH, of Priesthill, a Lieutenant of Mackay's Regiment, in Danish service 1626, in Swedish service 1629, wounded at Oldenburg. [TGSI.VIII.187]

ROSS, HUGH, a merchant in Gothenburg, Sweden, 1727. [JSL#271] [Goteborgs Landsarkivet]

ROSS, JOHN, second son of Zachary Ross of Hawk, a gentleman in St Thomas, Danish West Indies, matriculated at Glasgow University in 1804, graduated MD there in 1811. [MUG#209]

ROSS, Sir JOHN, the navigator and consul in Stockholm, Sweden, 1842. [NAS.GD18.3502/3536]

ROSS, NICHOLAS, a Captain of Mackay's Regiment, in Danish service 1626, in Swedish service 1629. [TGSI.VIII.187]

ROSS, ..., child of Thomas Ross, was buried in St Peter's, Malmo, Sweden, in 1564.[SAM]

RUAN, WILLIAM, a planter, died on 29 July 1735, probate St Jan, Danish West Indies. [RAK: 1826-1836, fos.236-252]

RUAN, WILLIAM, eldest son of William Ruan a merchant in St Croix, Danish West Indies, matriculated at Glasgow University in 1810, graduated MD from Edinburgh University in 1818, married Christian second daughter of William Dumbreck, South Coates, Edinburgh, at Hannah's Rest Estate, St Croix, on 16 February 1823, father of a daughter born in St Croix on 28 November 1824, died there on 29 November 1857. [BM#15/492][FH#152] [MUG#249] [EMG#57]

RUSSELL, THOMAS, a soldier of the 1st Company of Cockburn's Regiment, in Swedish service, 1609. [SIS#217]

RUTHERFORD, E., a soldier of the 3rd Company of Cockburn's Regiment, in Swedish service, 1609. [SIS#217]

RUTHERFORD, THOMAS, jr., a merchant in Sheffield, eldest son of Andrew Rutherford a merchant in Jedburgh, Roxburghshire, died in Christiansted, St Croix, Danish West Indies, on 22 November 1808. [SM#71/398][EA#4750]

RUTHVEN, ARCHIBALD, authorised to recruit 1600 men for service under the King of Sweden 1573. [NAS.PC1.7.69]

RUTHVEN, Sir PATRICK, (Pater Rotwein), born 1586, a soldier in the service of Sweden 1606-1609, fought in Livonia and Russia, Swedish Quartermaster General in 1615, Colonel of the Kalmar Regiment in 1623, knighted on the battlefield by Gustavus Adolphus, Commander of a Scots Regiment in Elbing and Memel 1629-1630, a Lieutenant General in the service of Gustavus Adolphus of Sweden, 1630s, defeated the Saxons at Domitz 1635, returned to Britain during 1636, a General under Charles I, appointed Earl of Forth and Brentford, died in Dundee on 2 February 1651. [Monifieth G/s][SHR.ix.47] [NAS.GD16.34.12][SIS#40]

SAMSON, THOMAS, son of Thomas Samson (1777-1856), died in St Croix, Danish West Indies. [Kilmarnock, Laigh g/s]

SANDERSON, ALEXANDER, from Dundee, was admitted as a burgess of Bergen, Norway, in 1615. [SAB]

SANDERSON, ALEXANDER, from Walls, Orkney, a burgess of Bergen, Norway, in 1622. [SAB][POAS.XIII.39]

SANDERSON, ANDREW, from St Andrews, Fife, a burgess of Bergen, Norway, in 1619. [SAB]

SANDERSON, EDWARD, from Orkney, a burgess of Bergen, Norway, in 1638. [SAB]

SANDERSON, THOMAS, from Orkney, a burgess of Bergen, Norway, in 1635. [SAB]

SANDERSON, WALTER, from Aberdeen, was admitted as a burgess of Bergen, Norway, in 1618. [SAB]

SANDERSON, WILLIAM, from Orkney, a burgess of Bergen, Norway, in 1626. [SAB]

SANDERSON, ..., from Orkney, a burgess of Bergen, Norway, in 1612. [POAS.XIII.39]

SANDERSON, ..., a cooper from Orkney, a burgess of Bergen, Norway, in 1619. [POAS.XIII.39]

SANDILAND, JAMES, (alias Jacob Sandelijn), master of the Scotch Dutchman, trading on the Delaware, New Sweden, 1638. [SDD]

SANDILANDS, BARTHOLEMEW, born in Bordeaux, France, a resident of Edinburgh, a Jacobite of Prince Charles Edward Stuart's Guard in 1745, escaped on the ....of North Ferry of Dundee, Captain James Wemyss, from Lunan Bay, Montrose, to Norway, landed in Bergen on 13 May 1746, settled in Gothenburg, Sweden, by 1747. [SHR.lxx.65][CM#3997]

SCHETKY, J. G. C., born 1748 in Stockholm, Sweden, arrived in Dover, England, in 1772, a music-maker in Edinburgh by 1798. [ECA.SL115.2.1/21]

SCOLLAY, MARGARET, in Norway, daughter of William Scollay in Hourston, Orkney, 1622. [NAS.RD43.II.206]

SCOLLAY, MICHAEL, a burgess of Bergen, Norway, 1636. [NAS.RS43.V.260]

SCOTT, ALBERT, (Albert Skotte), was buried in St Peter's, Malmo, Sweden, in 1578. [SAM]

SCOTT, DAVID, (David Skotte), a farm-servant at Imsland, near Stavanger, Norway, 1611. [SAS#104]

SCOTT, ELISABETH, probate 18 March 1778 Christiansted, Danish West Indies. [RAK: CCCL.VII.249]

SCOTT, GEORGE, probate 4 June 1777 Christiansted, Danish West Indies. [RAK: XC.VI.249]

SCOTT, GEORGE, a Methodist preacher in Sweden from 1830 to 1842. [SIS#72]

SCOTT, JAMES, (Jacob Skotte), was buried in St Peter's, Malmo, Sweden, in 1567. [SAM]

SCOTT, JAMES, (Jakob Skotte), settled in the Stavanger area of Norway during the 1580s, by 1602 a farmer at Finnvik, Norway. [SAS#104]

SCOTT, JAMES JAMIESON, (Jacob Jacobsen Schot), from Montrose, Angus, a burgess of Bergen, Norway, in 1694. [SAB]

SCOTT, JAMES, probate 1 May 1776 Christiansted, Danish West Indies. [RAK:CCL.IV.268]

SCOTT, JENS, (Jens Skotte), was buried in St Peter's, Malmo, Sweden, in 1582. [SAM]

SCOTT, JOHN, (Hans Skotte), was buried in St Peter's, Malmo, Sweden, in 1589. [SAM]

SCOTT, JOHN, from Aberdeen, settled in Norway by 1646. [ABL.III.44]

SCOTT, JOHN, a merchant in Montrose, a Jacobite in Ogilvy's Regiment 1745, Jacobite Deputy Governor of Montrose, escaped to Gothenburg, Sweden, in 1746. [GK#118][OR#48][LPR#320][SHR.lxx.65]

SCOTT, JOHN, sr., a merchant in Gothenburg, Sweden, around 1755. [Goteborgs Landarkivet]

SCOTT, Mrs MARGARET, wife of John Scott, (Hans Skotte), buried in St Peter's, Malmo, Sweden, during 1556. [SAM]

SCOTT, Captain ROBERT, probate 12 August 1772 Christiansted, Danish West Indies. [RAK: CXL.IV.33]

SCOTT, SARAH EDWARD, born 1878, third daughter of William Scott a fishcurer, died in Uddevella, Sweden, on 27 January 1885. [S#12972]

SCOTT, THOMAS, from Halsingborg, was buried in St Peter's, Malmo, Sweden, in 1565. [SAM]

SCOTT, WILLIAM, from Aberdeen, settled in Norway by 1646. [ABL.III.44]

SCOTT, ..., daughter of Andrew Scott, (Anders Skotte), was buried in St Peter's, Malmo, Sweden, in 1564. [SAM]

SCOTT, ..., child of Alexander Scott, (Sander Skotte), was buried in St Peter's, Malmo, Sweden, in 1566. [SAM]

SCOTT, ..., wife of William Scott, (Villem Skotte), was buried in St Peter's, Malmo, Sweden, in 1564. [SAM]

SCOTT & FRASER, merchants in Gothenburg, Sweden, trading with Scotland during 1770s. [Goteborgs Landsarkivet]

SEATON, ..., an Ensign of Mackay's Regiment, in Swedish service 1629, killed at Stralsund. [TGSI.VIII.188]

SEATTER, JAMES, a burgess of Bergen, Norway, husband of Marjory Tulloch, 1648. [NAS.RS43.VI.454]

SEMPILL, JOHN, in St Croix, Danish West Indies, 1790.
[Caribbeana#5/625]

SEMPLE, ..., an officer of Mackay's Regiment, in Danish
service 1626, in Swedish service 1629. [TGSI.VIII.189]

SENNOTT, WILLIAM, Major of Mackay's Regiment, in Danish
service 1626, in Swedish service 1629, died of the plague in
Stettin. [TGSI.VIII.186]

SETON, ALEXANDER, Lieutenant Colonel of Mackay's
Regiment, in Danish service 1626, in Swedish service 1629,
wounded at Oldenburg during October 1627. [TGSI.VIII.185]

SETON, JOHAN, (John Seton), an officer of the Danish Force in
Ireland, 1689-1691. [DFI#146]

SHEARER, JOHN, son of Thomas Shearer a burgess of
Aberdeen and his wife Agnes Mathewson, was admitted as
a burgess of Elsinore, Denmark, in 1593, dead by July 1597.
[MSC.II.26/39]

SHERIFF, JOHN, in St Thomas, Danish West Indies, eldest son of
Mathew Sheriff, tacksman of Captainhead, 1783.
[NAS.RD4.234.764]

SHERIFF, ROBERT, eldest son of Robert Sheriff a merchant in
Glasgow, educated at Glasgow University in 1819, a
merchant in New York, died on Diamond Estate, St Croix,
Danish West Indies, on 18 August 1847, testament
confirmed with the Commissariat of Edinburgh in 1859.
[NAS.SC70.1.101] [ANY.2.183]

SHIELS, JAMES, probate 1776 Christiansted, Danish West
Indies. [RAK: CCCX.VIII.133]

SIBBALD, DAVID, son of John Sibbald of Keir and his wife Janet
Strachan, a Lieutenant Colonel of the Swedish Army who
was killed in Germany during September 1641, birth brief
issued in 1642. [APB]

SIBBALD, JOHN, possibly from Edinburgh, a merchant in Gothenburg, Sweden, in 1768, trading with Scotland during 1770s. [NAS.RS27.181.101] [Goteborgs Landsarkivet]

SIMPSON, DAVID, and his wife Marie Lentron, from Dysart, Fife, then in Stockholm, Sweden, in 1688. [NAS.RD2.69.311]

SIMPSON, DUNCAN, probate 31 March 1773 Fredericksted, Danish West Indies. [RAK]

SINCLAIR, ANDREW, born 1614, to Sweden as a musketeer in Colonel Robert Stuart's Regiment during 1635, a Regimental commander by 1678, enobled in 1680, died in 1689. [SHR.IX.276]

SINCLAIR, DAVID, to Sweden in 1651, a Cavalry officer who was killed at the Battle of Warschau in 1656. [SHR.ix.275]

SINCLAIR, FRANCIS, son of James Sinclair of Murkle, a Major of Mackay's Regiment, in Danish service 1626, in Swedish service 1629, settled in Sweden, enobled there in 1645. [SHR.ix.275][TGSI.VIII.186]

SINCLAIR, HENRY or HENRIK, a customs inspector in Gothenburg, Sweden, around 1630. [SE#112]

SINCLAIR, JOHN, third son of George Sinclair, 5th Earl of Caithness, a Lieutenant Colonel of Mackay's Regiment in Swedish service, killed at Newmarke, Upper Palatinate, during 1632. [SHR.ix.51][TGSI.VIII.185]

SIOBLAD, Baroness CHARLOTTA CHRISTIAN, relict of Lord Kenneth Duffus, testament confirmed with the Commissariot of Edinburgh on 26 September 1778. [NAS]

SKEEN, MARY, died on 28 September 1819, probate St Jan, Danish West Indies. [RAK: 1807-1828]

SKENE, ELIZA, eldest daughter of James Skene of Rubislaw, Aberdeenshire, married Chevalier de Heidenstar, the Swedish Minister to the Greek Court, in Athens, Greece, on 5 March 1840. [EEC#20041]

SLATER, ROBERT ROBERTSON, from Orkney, a burgess of Bergen, Norway, in 1643, died 1683. [SAB]

SMART, JOHN, from Dundee, a burgess of Bergen, Norway, in 1639. [SAB]

SMELLIE, MIMA, fourth daughter of John Smellie a merchant in Edinburgh, and wife of Thomas Mackintosh, died in Ryd, Sweden, on 1 February 1885. [S#12973]

SMITH, JEAN, born in Fordyce, Banffshire, a housekeeper in Gothenborg, Sweden, from 1759, married Peter Engstrom, died in Sweden during 1821. [NS#7.1.147]

SMITH, ROBERT, a merchant in Stockholm, Sweden, in 1641, son of George Smith a merchant burgess of Edinburgh. [ECA.Moses.22/882/885]

SMITH, WILLIAM, a merchant in Christiansted, Danish West Indies, 1821. [NAS.RD5.204.550]

SMITH, WILLIAM JOHNSON, from Scotland, a burgess of Bergen, Norway, in 1672. [SAB]

SMYTH, ROBERT, a merchant burgess of Stockholm, Sweden, 1641. [NAS.GD172.1773/1774]

SMYTH, THOMAS, a leatherworker from Norway, settled in Edinburgh during 1657. [EBR.13.2.1657]

SNEJDAN, or ENGSTROM, MARGARET, in Gothenburg, Sweden, grand-daughter of John Henderson, an innkeeper in Wallacetown, 1818. [NAS.SH.10.2.1818]

SORENSEN, GEORGE WIGHT, fourth son of C. Marins Sorensen in Leith, was drowned in the Christianna Fiord, Norway, near Vallo on 29 July 1884. [S#12819]

SPALDING, GABRIEL, born 1659, a resident of Gothenburg, Sweden, son of the deceased John Spalding a Scot who settled in Gothenburg, applied to the Privy Council of Scotland for, and was granted, a birth-brief on 3 December 1674, died 1698. [RPCS.IV.306][SE#113]

SPALDING JAMES or JACOB, born 1625, settled in Gothenburg, Sweden, and later in Norrkoping, Sweden, died 1676.

SPALDING JOHN or HANS, born in Scotland, son of George Spalding and his wife Helena Ogilvie, settled as a merchant in Gothenburg, Sweden, died there in 1667. [Goteborgs Landsarkivet]

SPALDING, JOHN, representative of the Crown of Sweden in Dunkirk, France, son of the deceased John Spalding a Scot who settled in Gothenburg, Sweden, applied to the Privy Council of Scotland for, and was granted, a birth-brief on 3 December 1674. [RPCS.IV.306]

SPENCE, DAVID, son of John Spence in Kirkwall, Orkney, settled in Bergen, Norway, died before 1630. [NAS.GD31.37; RS43.4.129]

SPENS, COLIN, late servant to John Hall and Company, merchants in Gothenburg, Sweden, testament confirmed with the Commissariat of Edinburgh on 26 March 1783. [NAS]

SPENS, JAMES, third son of William Spens, to Sweden, a Swedish Army officer then Swedish Ambassador to England in 1612, licensed to recruit 1200 men in Scotland for Sweden, in Swedish service, 1624; died during 1632, will subscribed in Stockholm, Sweden, on 31 May 1631. [NAS.PC1.30.186][SIS#25] [SHR.IX.276][SS#25][NAS.GD334.114]

SPENS, JAMES, son of James Spens in Edinburgh, a drum-major in Swedish service in Doesburg, Riga, Amsterdam and Batavia from 1617 to 1632. [NAS.RH9.2.231/242]

SPINK, JOHN, born 1821, son of John Spink and his wife Barbara Carey, died on St Thomas, Danish West Indies, 17 August 1850. [Arbroath Abbey g/s]

STAIG, JOHN JAMIESON, from Scotland, a burgess of Bergen, Norway, in 1615. [SAB]

STANGER, JOHN, from Orkney, a cordiner in Bergen, Norway, 1644. [NAS.RS43.6.436]

STARK, WILLIAM, a shipmaster from Auchenvool(?), applied to be a burgess of Bergen, Norway, in 1711. [SAB]

STEEDMAN, ANN SARAH, second daughter of Dr William Steedman in St Croix, Danish West Indies, married Joseph Busby, in St Croix on 23 July 1823. [BM#14/623]

STEEDMAN, ELIZABETH, wife of Dr William Steedman, died in St Croix, Danish West Indies, on 20 September 1843. [GM.NS20.670]

STEEDMAN, LUCTRETIA GORDON, eldest daughter of Dr William Steedman in St Croix, Danish West Indies, died in Portobello, Edinburgh, on 1 March 1841. [GM.NS15/669]

STEEDMAN, WILLIAM, born on 13 June 1764 in Thurso, Caithness, second son of Thomas Steedman and his wife Anne Murray in Anderstown, educated at Glasgow University in 1782, a physician in St Croix, Danish West Indies, by 1790, married Elizabeth Gordon, daughter of the late Dr George Gordon of St Kitts, in Glasgow on 2 February 1795, died in St Croix on 7 April 1844. [SM.57.132] [MAGU#132][Caribbeana#4.17][GM.NS21.670]

STEENCULE, JOHAN, of the Society of Merchants of the Iceland and Faeroes Company of Copenhagen, Denmark, 1626. [NAS.RS43.III.465]

STEVENSON, ANDREW, master of the Hope of Trontheim, Norway, 1697.   [NAS.RD4.81.609]

STEWART, ALEXANDER, a soldier of 2nd Company of Cockburn's Regiment in Swedish service, 1609. [SIS#217]

STEWART, ANDREW, brother of the Earl of Traquair, a Lieutenant of Mackay's Regiment, in Danish service 1626, died during October 1627 after Oldenburg. [TGSI.VIII.188]

STEWART, FREDERICK, a soldier of 2nd Company of Cockburn's Regiment in Swedish service, 1609. [SIS#217]

STEWART, GEORGE, a Captain of Mackay's Regiment, in Danish service 1626, in Swedish service 1629, later Lieutenant Colonel of Conway's Regiment. [TGSI.VIII.187]

STEWART, HUGH, St Croix, Danish West Indies, died in Glasgow on 26 October 1826. [AJ#4115]

STEWART, JAMES, a soldier of 2nd Company of Cockburn's Regiment in Swedish service, 1609. [SIS#217]

STEWART, J., a Lieutenant of 2nd Company of Cockburn's Regiment in Swedish service, 1609. [SIS#217]

STEWART, JAMES, (Jacob Styffuert), from Orkney, a burgess of Bergen, Norway, in 1640. [SAB]

STEWART, JAMES, a burgess of Bergen, Norway, 1646. [NAS.SC11.5.1646/17]

STEWART, R., a Lieutenant of 1st Company of Cockburn's Regiment in Swedish service, 1609. [SIS#216]

STEWART, ROBERT, a Lieutenant of Mackay's Regiment, in Danish service 1626, in Swedish service, 1629, later Colonel of Lumsden's Pikemen. [TGSI.VIII.188]

STEWART, SIMON, son of Robert Stewart of Touccars, to Scandinavia in 1612, a Captain of the Swedish Navy in 1616, and an Admiral by 1630, died a landowner in Uppland, Sweden. [SIS#52]

STEWART, THOMAS, from Aberdeen, was admitted as a burgess of Bergen, Norway, in 1618. [SAB]

STEWART, THOMAS, councillor of Nya Lodose and later councillor and merchant of Gothenburg, Sweden, in 1624. [Goteborgs Landsarkivet][SIS#54]

STEWART, WILLIAM, brother of the Earl of Traquair, Lieutenant Colonel of Mackay's Regiment, in Swedish service, wounded at Oldenburg during October 1627. [SHR.IX.51][TGSI.VIII.185]

STEWART, WILLIAM, a merchant in Gothenburg, married Barbara, daughter of William King of Newmilne at Greyfriars near Elgin on 5 February 1763. [SM.25.118]

STEWART, WILLIAM, of Answanly, formerly a merchant in Gothenburg, Sweden, later in Elgin, Morayshire, 1765. [NAS.RS29.VII.389]

STOCKS, EDWARD, a Jacobite in 1745, settled in Gothenburg, Sweden, by 1747. [SHR.lxx.65]

STRACHAN, JAMES, a merchant in Bergen, Norway, and a burgess of Montrose, Angus, in 1764. [Montrose Burgess Roll]

STRATTON, WILLIAM, (Willum Straetten), a glover from Montrose, Angus, a burgess of Bergen, Norway, in 1657. [SAB]

STUART, ANDREW or ANDERS, commander of the Svenska Bjorn in 1598, a Rear Admiral of the Swedish Navy by 1621. [SIS#52]

STUART, HANS, son of John Stuart of Ochiltree, settled at Hedenlunda, Sweden, by 1582, Inspector General of foreign troops in Swedish service by 1609, married Brita Soop, died in 1618, buried in Vadsbro Church. [SIS#21]

STUART, JAMES, a Jacobite in 1745, settled in Gothenburg, Sweden, by 1747. [SHR.lxx.65]

STUART, JOSEPH, a Jacobite in 1745, settled in Gothenburg, Sweden, by 1747. [SHR.lxx.65]

STUART, J., a soldier of 1st Company of Cockburn's Regiment in Swedish service, 1609. [SIS#217]

SUTHERLAND, ..., a Lieutenant of Mackay's Regiment, in Danish service 1626, in Swedish service 1629, promoted in Ruthven's Regiment. [TGSI.VIII.188]

SUTTON, JOHN, in St Croix, Danish West Indies, father of Mary Sutton, 1756. [NAS.S/H]

SWENSEN, ANDERS, born in Gothenborg, Sweden, in 1760, settled in Fisherrow, Edinburgh, by 1788 as a servant to a Mrs Dickson. [ECA.SL115.2.1/91]

SYDSERF, PATRICK, sergeant major under Colonel James Ramsay of the Swedish Army in Germany, dead by May 1634. [NAS.NRAS.0028.8.1]

SYFS (?), STEPHEN, a shipmaster from Leven, Fife, applied to be a burgess of Bergen, Norway, in 1735. [SAB]

TAILYOUR, JAMES, a merchant in Gothenburg, Sweden, around 1745. [Goteborgs Landarkivet]

TAIT, WILLIAM, in Bergen, Norway, 1630. [NAS.RS43.4.117]

TAIT, W., a soldier of 2nd Company of Cockburn's Regiment in Swedish service, 1609. [SIS#217]

TARRAS, JOHN, born 16 March 1732, son of ....Tarras, a merchant in Banff, and his wife Margaret Gilchrist, settled in Gothenborg, Sweden, as a merchant, during 1758, married (2) Anna Margarita Augustin, died there on 5 May 1790. [NS#7.1.147][Goteborgs Landsarkivet]

TAYLOR, ALEXANDER, probate 1 November 1780, Christiansted, Danish West Indies. [RAK: L.XXXIX.278]

TAYLOR, THOMAS, a merchant in Bergen, Norway, and a nephew of Alexander Taylor in Kirkwall, Orkney, 1661. [NAS.SH.1661]

TAYLOR, WILLIAM, a burgess of Bergen, Norway, husband of Geils Paplay in Orkney, 1624. [NAS.RS43.3.219]

THOMASON, ALEXANDER, from Scotland, a burgess of Bergen, Norway, in 1614. [SAB]

THOMASON, JOHN, a weaver from Orkney, a burgess of Bergen, Norway, in 1671. [SAB]

THOMASON, THOMAS, from Orkney, a burgess of Bergen, Norway, in 1623. [POAS.XIII.39]

THOMPSON, ROBERT, in St Croix, Danish West Indies, 1790. [Caribbeana#5/265]

THOMPSON, SAMUEL, in St Croix, Danish West Indies, 1790. [Caribbeana#5/265]

THOMSON, ALEXANDER, from Dundee, was admitted as a burgess of Bergen, Norway, in 1618, dead by 1635. [SAB]

THOMSON, GEORGE, from Edinburgh, a burgess of Bergen, Norway, in 1641. [SAB]

THOMSON, JAMES, from Shetland, a burgess of Bergen, Norway, in 1608. [POAS.XIII.39]

THOMSON, JAMES, in Norkopping and Stockholm, Sweden,1684. [NAS.RH15.106.531]

THOMSON, JOHN, from St Andrews, Fife, admitted as a burgess of Bergen, Norway, in 1623. [SAB]

THOMSON, JOHN, a shoemaker from Orkney, a burgess of Bergen, Norway, in 1625. [SAB]

THOMSON, JOHN, a shipmaster from Prestonpans, applied to be a burgess of Bergen, Norway, in 1695. [SAB]

THOMSON, MAGNUS, from Orkney, a burgess of Bergen, Norway, in 1623. [SAB]

THOMSON, MAGNUS, a weaver from Orkney, a burgess of Bergen, Norway, in 1641. [SAB]

THOMSON, PATRICK, a merchant in Stockholm, Sweden,1672. [NAS.RH15.106/147]

THOMSON, PETER, from Orkney, a burgess of Bergen, Orkney, in 1640. [SAB]

THOMSON, or SMITH, ROBERT, a resident of Elsinore, Denmark, husband of Janet Gilchrist, from Dundee, 3 July 1556. [DCA.Court Book#III]

THOMSON, STEPHEN, son of John Thomson and his wife Margaret Elder in Brigend, a weaver in Elsinore, Denmark, around 1607. [Dundee Archives, CB.III/69]

THOMSON, THOMAS, from Orkney, a burgess of Bergen, Norway, in 1624. [SAB]

THOMSON, WILLIAM, from Peterhead, Aberdeenshire, a burgess of Bergen, Norway, in 1692. [SAB]

THOMSON, WILLIAM, probate 14 January 1762 Christiansted, Danish West Indies. [RAK]

THORBURN, WILLIAM, in Karsam, Sweden, 5 July 1832. [NAS.RD.Renfrew, #13/78]

THORNTON, JOHN, died 29 August 1752, probate 19 November 1760 Christiansted also St Croix, Danish West Indies. [RAK: 1747-1782, fo.182]

THORNTON, THOMAS JOHNSON, from Dundee, a burgess of Bergen, Norway, in 1614. [SAB]

THORNTON, ..., son of Edward Thornton, was born in Stockholm on 2 August 1816. [SM#78.798]

THUACH, JOHN JOHNSON, from Scotland, a burgess of Bergen, Norway, in 1619. [SAB]

TODD, ALEXANDER, a merchant in Gothenburg, Sweden, 1727. [JSL#271]

TODD, DAVID, a shipmaster from Kirkcaldy, Fife, a burgess of Bergen, Norway, in 1692. [SAB]

TODD, JAMES, in St Croix, Danish West Indies, 1790. [Caribbeana#5/265]

TOLLER, DAVID, from Aberdeen, a burgess of Bergen, Norway, in 1631. [SAB]

TOMMASON, MAGNUS, from Orkney, a burgess of Bergen, Norway, 1623. [POAS.XIII.39]

TOTTIE, C. W., from Aberdeenshire, a merchant in Stockholm, Sweden, during 1770s. [NS.11.1]

TOTTIE, THOMAS, born in Jedburgh, Roxburghshire, in 1664, emigrated to Sweden in 1688, a tobacco dresser in Stockholm from the 1690s, died in 1724. [SIS#63]

TOWER, ALEXANDER, born 15 July 1801, son of George Tower and his wife Euphemia Sutherland in Aberdeen, educated at King's College, Aberdeen, from 1815 to 1819, then a planter in St Croix, Danish West Indies. [KCA.2.243]

TOWER, ANN, born 1792, eldest daughter of John Tower in St Croix, Danish West Indies, died in Ferryhill, Aberdeen, on 5 April 1814. [AJ#3457]

TOWER, ANN, from Edinburgh, died in St Croix, Danish West Indies, on 8 January 1843. [NAS.Est,Def.C2078]

TOWER, JAMES, in St Croix, Danish West Indies, 1776. [NLS.Acc8793/30]

TOWER, JAMES, MD, in St Thomas, Danish West Indies, 1804. [KCA#2/395]

TOWER, JOHN, a merchant in St Croix, Danish West Indies, 1784. [NAS.RD3.244.530]; late of St Croix, died in Aberdeen on 13 April 1799. [SM#61/284][EA#3696][St Nicholas g/s, Aberdeen]

TOWER, JOHN, son of James Tower, MD, in St Thomas, Danish West Indies, was educated at King's College, Aberdeen, in 1804. [KCA#2/395]

TRAILL, ISABELLA, relict of Christopher Thuring in Helsingfors, Sweden, 1839. [NAS.GD31.513/4]

TRAILL, MARTIN, in Uplso, Norway, testament confirmed with the Commissariat of Edinburgh on 26 September 1643. [NAS]

TRIVERIC, CHARLES, Count de Piper, born 1783 in Stockholm, a Swedish officer, formerly in Vienna, Austria, arrived at Harwich on 24 March 1805, residing in Edinburgh. [ECA.SL115.2.2/46]

TROUP, ALEXANDER, Major of the Swedish Army, Commandant of Brix, 1635-1653. [NAS.GD57.336]

TROUP, PATRICK, a Lieutenant in Danish service, 1627. [RPCS.15.6.1627][HG.III.407]

TULLOCH, ALEXANDER, a Captain of Mackay's Regiment, in Danish service 1626, in Swedish service, 1629. [TGSI.VIII.187]

TURNBULL, A., a soldier of 2nd Company of Cockburn's Regiment in Swedish service, 1609. [SIS#217]

TURNBULL, JAMES, (Jacob Tromle), from Lester (Lybster?) Scotland, a burgess of Bergen, Norway, in 1641. [SAB]

TURNBULL, MERRICK, probate 1750 St Croix, Danish West Indies. [RAK]

URQUHART, GORDON, born in Rosskeen on 23 February 1788, son of Reverend Thomas Urquhart and his wife Johanna Clunes, a Lieutenant of the 96th Regiment, died in St Croix, Danish West Indies, on 5 September 1808. [F.7.68]

VON SPRUNGUPUIL, JOST, a merchant in Bergen, Norway, 1697. [NAS.RD2.80.2.613]

WADE ANDREW AFFLECK, probate 27 February 1767 Fredericksted, Danish West Indies. [RAK]

WADE, GEORGE, probate 30 September 1769 Fredericksted, Danish West Indies. [RAK]

WADE, THOMAS, probate 30 September 1769 Fredericksted, Danish West Indies. [RAK]

WALDIE, JAMES, a merchant in Bergen, Norway, was admitted as a burgess of Montrose, Angus, in 1728. [Montrose Burgess Roll]

WALKER, JOHN, probate 31 March 1769 Fredericksted, Danish West Indies. [RAK]

WALKER, JOHN, born in Aberdeenshire, settled in St Croix, Danish West Indies, died in Glasgow on 11 July 1809. [SM#71/560]

WALKER, ROBERT, died in St Thomas, Danish West Indies, on 10 May 1813. [AJ#3422][EA#5173/130]

WALKER, THOMAS, a surgeon from Kinross, married Jean, daughter of James McAra a merchant in Largs, Ayrshire, in St Thomas, Danish West Indies, during 1813. [EA#5134/13]

WALLACE, ALEXANDER, HM Consul in Bergen, Norway, and a burgess of Montrose, Angus, in 1749. [Montrose Burgess Roll]

WALLACE, GEORGE, a merchant from Banff, applied to be a burgess of Bergen, Norway, in 1711. [SAB]; a merchant in Bergen,1715. [NAS.RD4.117.1052]

WALLACE, JAMES, a merchant from Banff, applied to be a burgess of Bergen, Norway, in 1727. [SAB]

WALLACE, JOHN, son of Alexander Wallace in Bergen, Norway, was admitted as a burgess of Montrose in 1764. [Montrose Burgess Roll]

WALLACE, THOMAS, a soldier of 1st Company of Cockburn's Regiment in Swedish service, 1609. [SIS#217]

WALTERS, HENRY, from Scotland, was admitted as a burgess of Bergen, Norway, in 1625. [SAB]

WALTERSON, ALBERT, from Orkney, a burgess of Bergen, Norway, in 1631. [SAB]

WARDROP, D., a soldier of 1st Company of Cockburn's Regiment in Swedish service, 1609. [SIS#217]

WATERSTONE, HANS or JOHN, a burgher and merchant of Linkoping, Sweden, around 1579, a merchant in Stockholm, Sweden, in 1582, trading illegally in Vadstena in 1579 and in 1587, an officer in Livonia in the 1590s. forfeited his estate in Vadstena in 1608. [SIS#23]

WATSON, JOHN, sailor aboard the Enhiorningen, master Jens Munk, from Copenhagen on 9 May 1619 bound for Hudson's Bay, arrived there on 7 September 1619, died there 6 May 1620. [DCB]

WATSON, JOHN, probate 14 March 1781 Christiansted, Danish West Indies. [RAK: CCC.XXVI.168]

WATSON, WILLIAM, (Villem Wattsen), buried in St Peter's, Malmo, Sweden, in 1560. [SAM]

WATT, ALEXANDER, from Banff, settled in Copenhagen, Denmark, by 1832. [NAS.SH.1832]

WATT, WILLIAM, son of Robert Scott and his wife Helen Mylne in Pilmour, a weaver from Dundee who settled in Copenhagen, Denmark, before 1575. [Dundee Archives, CBIII]

WAUCHOPE, GILBERT, Captain of the Swedish Army, from Leith to Sweden in 1607. [RPCS.VII.420]

WAUCHOPE, JOHN, brother of the above Gilbert, from Leith to Sweden in 1607. [RPCS.VII.420]

WELCH, FRANCIS, a planter, died 9 December 1745, husband of Anna ....., probate 30 February 1747 St Croix, Danish West Indies. [RAK:1741-1748, fo.320]

WELCH, JOHN, husband of Eleanora ....., probate 30 February 1747 St Croix, Danish West Indies. [RAK]

WEMYSS, DAVID, a merchant of Dundee, to Gothenburg, Sweden, around 1650. [NAS.Parliamentary Papers, Vol.7.11.122]

WHIST, ALEXANDER, a Jacobite in 1745, settled in Gothenburg, Sweden, by 1747. [SHR.lxx.65]

WHITE, JAMES, probate 5 January 1780 Christiansted, Danish West Indies. [RAK.CCCC.IX.326]

WHITE, JOHN, probate 31 August 1768 Christiansted, Danish West Indies. [RAK]

WIDACK, JAMES, in Bergen, Norway, 1631. [NAS.RS43.IV.304]

WIDACK, JAMES, in Bergen, Norway, 1633. [NAS.RS43.IV.304]

WILLIAMSON, ALEXANDER, from Orkney, a burgess of Bergen, Norway, in 1648. [SAB]

WILLIAMSON, ANDREW, from Largo, Fife, applied to become a burgess of Bergen, Norway, in 1641. [SAB]

WILLIAMSON, EDWARD, from Kirkwall, Orkney, a burgess of Bergen, Norway, in 1648. [SAB]

WILLIAMSON, JEREMY, from Orkney, a burgess of Bergen, Norway, in 1617. [SAB][POAS.XIII.39]

WILLIAMSON, JOHN, from Scotland, a burgess of Bergen, Norway, in 1621. [SAB]

WILLIAMSON, JOHN, a cooper from Orkney, a burgess of Bergen, Norway, in 1616. [POAS.XIII.39]

WILLIAMSON, JOHN, from Orkney, a burgess of Bergen, Norway, in 1639. [SAB]

WILLIAMSON, MAGNUS, from Kirkcaldy, Fife, a burgess of Bergen, Norway, in 1619. [SAB]

WILLIAMSON, MAGNUS, from Orkney, a burgess of Bergen, Norway, in 1622. [SAB][POAS.XIII.39]

WILLIAMSON, MAGNUS, from Scotland, a burgess of Bergen,

Norway, in 1633. [SAB]

WILLIAMSON, OLIVER, from Shetland, a burgess of Bergen, Norway, in 1593. [POAS.XIII.39]

WILLIAMSON, ROBERT, (Robbertt Villumbsen), from Arbroath, Angus, a burgess of Bergen, Norway, in 1630. [SAB]

WILLIAMSON, ROBERT, from Orkney, a burgess of Bergen, Norway, in 1638. [SAB]

WILLIAMSON, THOMAS, from Kirkwall, Orkney, a burgess of Bergen, Norway, in 1613. [SAB]

WILLIAMSON, WILLIAM, from Orkney, a burgess of Bergen, Norway, in 1597. [POAS.XIII.39]

WILLIAMSON, WILLIAM, from Dundee, a burgess of Bergen, Norway, in 1614. [SAB]

WILLIAMSON, WILLIAM, a wright or joiner from Orkney, a burgess of Bergen, Norway, in 1620. [SAB][POAS.XIII.39]

WILLIAMSON, WILLIAM, from Orkney, a burgess of Bergen, Norway, in 1628. [SAB]

WILLIAMSON, ..., from Orkney, a burgess of Bergen, Norway, in 1613. [POAS.XIII.39]

WILSON, JOHN FLEMING, eldest son of George Wilson, late of Martin and Wilson, died in St Croix, Danish West Indies, on 2 February 1868. [S#7791]

WILSON, ..., Major of Mackay's Regiment, in Danish service 1626, in Swedish service 1629. [TGSI.VII.186]

WINTON, GILBERT, from Dundee, a burgess of Bergen, Norway, in 1640. [SAB]

WOOD, WILLIAM, probate 31 December 1778 Fredericksted, Danish West Indies. [RAK: fo.305]

WRIGHT, ROBERT, probate 1774 Christiansted, Danish West Indies. [RAK:CCL.XXV.391]

WYLLY, THOMAS, died on 5 May 1778, probate Christiansted, Danish West Indies. [RAK: 1769-1780, fo.142]

YOUNG, ALEXANDER, settled in Elsinore, Denmark, dead by 1560. [Dundee Archives, Court Book IV/104]

YOUNG, ALEXANDER, a merchant from Montrose, applied to become a burgess of Bergen, Norway, in 1704. [SAB]

YOUNG, GILBERT, (Gilbert Jung), was buried in St Peter's, Malmo, Sweden, on 25 August 1591. [SAM]

YOUNG, JOHN or HANS, a town councillor of Gothenburg, Sweden, in 1624. [Goteborgs Landsarkivet]

YOUNG, JOHN, probate 28 February 1767 Christiansted, Danish West Indies. [RAK: XXXI]

YOUNG, WILLIAM, probate 1767 Christiansted, Danish West Indies. [RAK: V.III.11]